W9-ADD-082

THE CITY OF GOD
AND THE CITY OF
MAN IN AFRICA

DT 779.7
B7

THE CITY
OF GOD
AND THE
CITY OF MAN
IN AFRICA

by Edgar H. Brookes
and Amry Vandenbosch

UNIVERSITY OF KENTUCKY PRESS

1966

105538

APR

Copyright (c) 1964 by the University of Kentucky Press
Printed in the United States of America by the
University of Kentucky Printing Division
Library of Congress Catalog Card
No. 64-13998

*The publication of this book has been made possible in
part through a grant from the Margaret Voorhies Haggin
Trust, established in memory of her husband, James Ben
Ali Haggin.*

PREFACE

DR. Edgar H. Brookes, professor emeritus of history
and political science at the University of Natal, in May,
1963, gave a series of two lectures at the University of
Kentucky which made a deep impression on those who
heard them. It was felt that these unique and moving
lectures should be made available to the large public
which is now so deeply interested in the developments in
that turbulent African continent. The publishers suggested
that a background piece for each of the highly interpre-
tive essays by Professor Brookes would be helpful to

many readers; I was asked to contribute these chapters. While I felt highly honored to be associated with Dr. Brookes in this enterprise, it was with some reluctance that I agreed to do so, as any contribution from me would detract from the unusual quality of the essays by him.

The reader of the chapters by Dr. Brookes will quickly note a spiritual kinship between him and Alan Paton. These two men are leading representatives of a small band of noble, courageous, and patriotic South Africans. They are leaders of the Liberal Party which advocates the abandonment of *apartheid* and the extension of suffrage to all regardless of race.

A grateful acknowledgment is made of the generosity of Mr. and Mrs. Paul Blazer of Ashland, who through the Blazer Lecture Fund made possible the visit of Professor Brookes to our campus. I wish to express my thanks to the Social Science Research Council of New York and the University of Kentucky Research Fund for financial grants which made it possible for me to visit Africa in 1962.

Amry Vandenbosch

Lexington, Kentucky
November 11, 1963.

ONE

UNTIL a few years ago Africa, of which Professor Brookes so eloquently speaks in the next chapter, was an unknown continent. Today it is probably the most publicized region in the world. The uniformity given it by French green and British red now gone, the new Africa must be charted in many hues, some close on the color wheel, some far apart. For Africa's population is by no means homogeneous. Its 250 million inhabitants are divided racially, linguistically, culturally, religiously, and politically. This is quite to be expected, since Africa is a vast continent. It has an area of 11.5 million square miles, which is about 12 percent larger than North America. In such an extension of territory there is naturally a wide variety of climate, soil, and agricultural production, and of cultures and interests.

Geographically Africa is divided into several regions. There is the belt of land in northern Africa which is a part of the Mediterranean world and supports a considerable population. It is cut off from the rest of the continent by the great Sahara desert, which is virtually without inhabitants. There is a second, smaller desert and semidesert area in the southwest, embracing the sparsely populated but much disputed territory of South-West Africa, the Protectorate of Bechuanaland, and parts of Angola and South Africa. A grassland belt extending across the continent south of the Sahara desert represents a third region, and a tropical rain-forest area embracing the Congo River basin and the coastal plains of west Africa constitute a fourth. And lastly, there is the mass of mountains and high plateaus stretching from Ethiopia southward all the way to the Cape of Good Hope. This region enjoys a temperate climate, even though most of it is situated in the tropical zone, and has attracted considerable numbers of white settlers.

Although the peoples of Africa in racial origin are

almost entirely Negroid or Caucasoid, they are divided into innumerable tribes and language groups. About two-thirds of the population speaks Negritic and one-third Hamitic and Semitic languages. The former are found in central, or tropical, and southern Africa; the latter in Ethiopia, the Sahara region, and the northern part of the continent. Tropical Africa is often spoken of as "Black Africa." Arabic is dominant from Morocco to Sudan, but it and Swahili are the only languages spoken over a wide area. The latter is the lingua franca for more than ten million people and has official status in Kenya, Tanganyika, and the Republic of the Congo. No other language is used by more than six or seven million people. There were over five million Europeans in the whole of Africa in 1960. Since then, many of the Europeans in Morocco, Algeria, and Tunisia have left, as well as many of the white settlers in east Africa. About three and a half million Europeans and about a million and a half "Coloured" (mixed Europeans and Bantus) live in South Africa. There is a considerable body of Indians in Africa, chiefly in the east and south, with 500,000 in the Republic of South Africa alone. About 100,000 Arabs also live in east Africa, half of them on the island of Zanzibar.

Africa is also sharply divided religiously. About half of the peoples of the continent still adhere to their native animist religions. Some 80 million are Moslems. Islamism has long been the religion of North Africa, but it has also penetrated south of the Sahara, where there are now some 40 million adherents. Estimates as to the number of Christians vary greatly, with 40 million as the upper figure.

Politically, Africa is divided into about forty political entities or administrative units. Nigeria, with about 37 million people, has the largest population, followed by the United Arab Republic with 27 million and Ethiopia with some 20 million. The majority of the African states have populations running from a half to five or six million.

Egypt and the northern fringe of Africa are old in the history of civilization. Northern Africa was a part of the Roman Empire and, like Rome itself, was conquered by the barbarians from the north. This Africa produced St. Augustine, a great theologian, a distinguished philosopher, and one of the greatest of the church fathers. Some interesting comparisons can be drawn between the Africa of St. Augustine and that of today. The Africa of the fifth century was in turmoil, as is the Africa of today, but the disturbances in the earlier period were caused by the invasion of northern Africa by the Vandals of Europe, while Africa today is in an unsettled state because it is in the process of throwing off the political domination of the Europeans. Christianity in northern Africa was displaced by Islamism; many centuries after the Bishop of Hippo, however, it was reintroduced into the continent, this time south of the Sahara, and today it is a viable influence. Islamism too has spread southward, and northern Africa, like the rest of the continent, is undergoing profound change, if not renewal, and has become less associated with Europe and more closely identified with the main currents of Africa as a whole.

A few other facts about Africa should be noted at the outset. In spite of the rising tide of nationalism since World War II, tribal loyalties are still disturbingly strong. They constitute a serious obstacle to political integration. Illiteracy is still very high; probably not over 25 percent of the adult population can read and write. Levels of production and consumption are very low, among the lowest of the world. About three-quarters of Africa's population is engaged in agriculture, compared with less than one-tenth in the United States.

The attitude of the Western world toward Africa has for centuries had strange aspects. At the door of Europe geographically, Africa was not thought of as a continent until the middle of the nineteenth century. Egypt always was regarded as an Asian rather than an African land. The north coast of Africa in ancient times was associated with Europe, and after the conquest of the region by

Islamism it was considered an extension of the Middle East. For the European, only the western rim of Africa had any significance, and that only after the discovery of America. The east coast was part of the world of the Indian Ocean; it became more Arab and Asian than the west coast became European. The southern tip of Africa became important as a refreshing station for European ships on the long cruise to and from India, Java, and the Far East. The establishment of the settlement at Cape Town in 1652 points up the fact that for several centuries Africa was regarded by Europeans as an obstruction on the way to India and eastern Asia.

With the exploration of the interior by the missionary-explorer David Livingstone, Africa came to be regarded as a continent. How is it that Africa, which had within its borders Egypt known throughout history as a cradle of civilization, should so long remain the unknown, the Dark Continent? Why did not the West penetrate this continent so close at hand?

A number of reasons have been advanced to explain this strange phenomenon. Africa could not easily be penetrated because its great rivers were blocked to navigation near their mouths. Had the Congo, for example, been navigable into the interior, the story would have been different. Large inlets from the sea generally provide good harbors, but nature treated Africa niggardly in this respect. Sub-Sahara Africa was feared because of its deadly diseases. The interior was regarded as having a very hostile environment for the white man. It has also been asserted that Europeans did not penetrate the interior for the reason that Africa produced nothing for trade, except slaves, and they were delivered at the coastal towns by African and Arab slave traders. Thus there was no need to establish more than trading posts on the coast. The extensive trade in the one article in which the West was interested contributed to the backwardness of its people. For years the cruel traffic drained Africa of its manpower. It is estimated that as many as twenty million Africans were transported to the Americas between the sixteenth and nineteenth centuries.[1] With the outlawry of slave traffic, Europe had very little interest in Africa for nearly a century.

In a final outbreak of Western imperialism, Africa was brought under the political domination of Europe in the last quarter of the last century. Once the movement began, there was a scramble and at times bitter contention. Most of Africa had hardly moved beyond tribalism, so that the establishment of Western colonies brought about the

[1]Vernon McKay, *Africa in World Politics* (New York, 1963), p. 4, quoting figures from J. D. Fage, *Introduction to the History of West Africa.*

first substantial administrative and political unification. Colonialism diffused the advances made in the West in education, science, technology, government, and administration. In fact, it was this diffusion which undermined colonialism. The forces which had stimulated the nationalist spirit in the West began to produce similar effects in the dependencies. When Christian churches began missionary activities and capitalists began investing in business enterprises in the colonies, the total culture of the West was introduced into African societies. An acceleration of the development of nationalism was the inevitable result. Insofar as there are nations in Africa today, they are the result of Western colonialism. The political boundary lines follow the colonial pattern.

If Africa was the last of the continents to be colonized by the West, it was also the last to be freed from dependent status. With the decolonization of Africa that remarkable and important phenomenon of modern history, the subjection of a vast part of the world to Western control, came to an end. Its liquidation came earlier and occurred more rapidly than was generally foreseen. The transition from colony to independent state in most cases took place smoothly, but in one important dependency it precipitated a convulsion which shocked the world.

Before 1910 there were only two independent countries

in all of this vast continent – Ethiopia and Liberia. Except for the brief Italian interlude from 1935 to 1941, the former has been independent since ancient times, while the latter came into existence in 1847, the result of a settlement of freed slaves from the United States which was established with the aid of American colonization societies. In 1910 the newly created Union of South Africa was granted self-government, and by the end of World War I it had virtually acquired control of its foreign relations and became an original member of the League of Nations. It was, however, controlled politically, and in every other way, by a small white minority. In 1922 Egypt became independent, but it is oriented more toward the Arab world than toward the whole of Africa, as its current name, United Arab Republic, suggests. The same may be said for Libya, which was granted independence in 1951, and for Morocco and Tunisia, which joined the ranks of independent states in 1956.

The achievement of independence by Sudan in 1956 marked the beginning of the decolonization of Black Africa, though the character of the population of the northern half of this country, as well as of those in political control, is Middle East. Beginning with Ghana in 1957, most of the colonies of tropical Africa became independent in rapid succession. Guinea followed in 1958, and in 1960 no fewer than sixteen former dependencies became members of the United Nations after achieving independence. Three more joined the roll of members in 1961, four in 1962, and two in 1963. Northern and Southern Rhodesia and Nyasaland will in all probability follow soon after. There will then remain only two dependencies with a population of over a million–the Portuguese territories of Angola and Mozambique. The future of eleven lesser territories is highly uncertain.

A number of factors are responsible for the rapid liquidation of colonialism in Africa and the end of colonialism in general. World War I marked the beginning of a change of attitude on the part of the Africans toward their white rulers. Many were taken far from their homes to participate in military campaigns in Africa and Europe, to fight with white men against other white men. They came to see Europeans in a different light, they acquired knowledge of the white man's world, and they developed sophistication. This experience engendered a sense of equality. This spirit was further stimulated by President Woodrow Wilson when he included in the Fourteen Points, as the "only possible" program for world peace, the necessity for the "strict observance" of the principle that in adjusting colonial claims "the interests of the populations concerned must have equal weight with the equitable claims

of the government whose title is to be determined."
Wilson's principle would now be wholly unacceptable,
since it equated the claims of the colonial powers with
those of the dependent peoples, but at the time it represented a marked advance and strengthened anticolonial
forces. The effect of all of this on the mind of many Africans was profound. It made them more race-conscious
and increased their self-respect.

What the war did in the form of shock treatment, education and missionary activities had long been doing in
a more gradual and better way. The teaching of Christianity that all men are equal in the sight of God especially tended to equalize the relations between the races.

The mandates system between the wars also played a
part in changing the attitude of Africans. Germany's colonies were not returned to her, nor annexed by the con-
querors, but placed under the administration of the latter
subject to international supervision, with the obligation to
govern them in accordance with "the principle that the
well-being and development of such peoples form a sacred
trust of civilization." The mandated territories in Africa
had an area of about 950,000 square miles and a population in 1926 of more than 13,000,000. The mandates
system had its shortcomings, but it did much to establish
the principle that the administration of dependencies had

ceased to be a purely national concern, and it prodded the mandatory, and indirectly all colonial powers, to more liberal policies. Moreover, the system looked toward the ultimate independence of all but the "C" mandates.

The announcement by the British in an official white paper in 1923, that where the interests of immigrants conflicted with those of the natives, the latter must prevail, strengthened the liberal trends. This statement of policy, which came to be known as paramountcy, emerged from the situation in Kenya, where the interests of immigrant Europeans and Indians had come into conflict.

The growing interest in Africa in the two decades between the wars was reflected in the new emphasis on African studies and the publication of several significant volumes. In 1921 there appeared *The Dual Mandate in British Tropical Africa*, by Sir F. D. (later Lord) Lugard, a British colonial official in Africa, and in 1928 Raymond L. Buell's comprehensive two-volume study, *The Native Problem in Africa.* Lord Hailey's monumental *An African Survey: A Study of Problems Arising in Africa South of the Sahara*, was published in 1938.[2]

The world was made very conscious of the colonial problem by the drive by Germany for the return of the colonies of which she had been deprived by the Treaty

[2] A new edition of this important work was published in 1957 in New York.

of Versailles in 1919. With the world depression and the rise of Hitler the German campaign became loud and insistent. The whole issue was cleverly simplified by the catching slogan of "The Haves and the Have-Nots." Hitler made colonial revision one of his chief demands.

World War II heightened anticolonial sentiment. The occupation by Japan of the dependencies of southeast Asia brought the problem of colonialism into sharp focus. The prestige of the white man had been seriously damaged, and the peoples of the occupied colonies bitterly opposed any suggestions of a return to their former colonial status after liberation from Japan. In the propaganda to combat Hitler's racism were implicit promises of a new day and an end of colonialism. The Atlantic Charter, which was the nearest counterpart to the Fourteen Points of World War I, contained a vague reference to the colonial problem in the third principle, in which the president of the United States and the prime minister of the United Kingdom declared that "they respect the right of all peoples to choose the form of government under which they will live."

The United Nations converted the mandates system into a stronger trusteeship system. The Trusteeship Council was given the power to send missions to the trust territories, a power which the Mandates Commission had sought but never obtained. Moreover, the council was composed of government representatives and not of independent specialists, as was the case of the Mandates Commission. The Charter also contained a declaration regarding non-self-governing territories, under which all members with dependencies undertook to administer them in accordance with the lofty principles laid down in the statement. Of great significance was the provision of Article 73 (e) under which the colonial powers agreed to transmit annual reports on social and economic conditions in their respective dependent territories. This innocent-looking provision gave the excuse for the General Assembly to discuss the administration of colonial territories and, indeed, the whole colonial question.

Increasing pressure on colonialism after World War II came especially from two sources, namely, the cold war between the West and the Communist world and the large increase in the membership of the United Nations, chiefly of former dependencies. The colonial issue offered the Communists a rare opportunity to embarrass the Western powers; the Soviet Union took full advantage of it. In the General Assembly, the Security Council, and the Trusteeship Council, Russia attacked bitterly all forms of colonialism and posed as the ardent friend of all dependent and underdeveloped peoples. It was difficult for the colonial powers to resist the pressure thus exerted against them.

FIFTEEN

With the enlargement of the membership of the United Nations the forces of anticolonialism became steadily stronger. The number of United Nations members has more than doubled since its formation in 1945, and the majority of the new members are former dependencies, almost all of whom suffer from a sense of grievance against the West. The so-called Afro-Asian Bloc is now the largest group in the General Assembly. It is divided on many issues, but on anything touching colonialism its members stand united. The anticolonial movement registered a great triumph in a sweeping declaration adopted by the General Assembly on December 14, 1960, by a vote of 89 to none, with nine abstentions. The declaration condemned "the subjection of peoples to alien subjugation, domination and exploitation," and asserted that "inadequacy of political, economic, social or education preparedness should never serve as a pretext for delaying independence." It demanded that "immediate steps ... be taken ... to transfer all powers to the peoples of (dependent) territories, without any conditions or reservations, in accordance with their freely expressed will and desire, without any distinction as to race, creed or color, in order to enable them to enjoy complete independence and freedom."

To further the implementation of the declaration, the General Assembly created a seventeen-member committee.

SIXTEEN

This Special Committee on Colonialism has been very active. It has directed the full force of the anticolonial feeling against the Portuguese and the white-dominated territories in southern Africa.

Hand in hand with the growth of anticolonialism was the development of nationalism in Africa. There was little manifestation of the new ferment in the two decades between the wars, but these were the formative years. Even before World War I, Christian missions had been quietly at work preparing the ground for the growth of nationalism. Missionaries went into the villages and the bush and introduced Western attitudes and ways of living. They also brought education. Before the missionaries came, only four out of hundreds of different languages had a native script. In order that the people might have the Bible, missionaries set to work to translate it into African languages. As a result, the entire Bible has been translated into more than twenty-five African languages and the New Testament into seventy; several hundred languages have been reduced to writing.

The teachings of the Bible, especially that of the unique worth and dignity of the individual in the sight of God, had a profound influence on the African. They released him from superstition and tradition and gave him a new status as an individual. The effect in the end was to stimulate the sentiment of nationalism. The influence of the distribution and teaching of the Bible on these important attitudes is sharply put by Ndabaningi Sithole, an African Christian and nationalist: "It is inconceivable to a logical mind that the Bible could deliver the African from traditional domination without at the same time redeeming him from colonial domination. If the Bible teaches that the individual is unique, of infinite worth before God, colonialism, in many respects, says just the opposite; so that in actual practice, Biblical teachings are at variance with colonialism, and it becomes only a matter of time before one ousts the other. The Bible-liberated African is now reasserting himself not only over tribal but also over colonial authority, since these two are fundamentally the same."[3]

The vision of the City of God which Africans received from the Bible made them determined to acquire the freedom to realize their vision of the City of Man. Unfortunately, African nationalism was fed by grievances as well as stimulated by aspirations. Africans feel very strong-

---

[3]*African Nationalism* (London, 1959), p. 53. Sir Andrew Cohen, former governor of Uganda, pays the following tribute to the work of Christian missions: "The contribution of missionaries to the progress of Africa cannot, I think, be fully grasped unless one has lived there, seen what they have built, and realized the leadership they have provided, the ideas and the moral values they have implanted and cultivated in these countries." *British Policy in Changing Africa* (Evanston, Ill., 1959), p. 8.

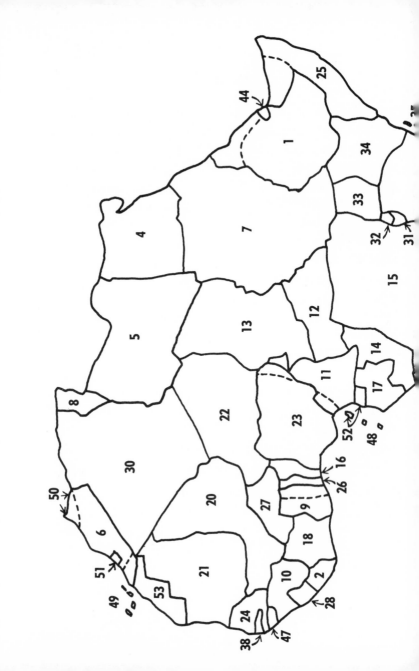

THE STATES AND TERRITORIES OF AFRICA, JANUARY 1, 1964

——— Boundaries of African states and dependent territories of European states

– – – Boundaries of dependent territories of African states

For names and explanatory notes, see the following table, keyed to the numbers on the map.

The States and Territories of Africa, January 1, 1964

Independent before 1960

1	Ethiopia	Ancient. Former trust territory of Eritrea added in 1952
2	Liberia	1847
3	South Africa	1910. Administers South-West Africa, former League of Nations mandate, with Walvis Bay
4	United Arab Republic	1922. Formerly called Egypt
5	Libya	1951. Former British-French trust territory
6	Morocco	1956. Former French and Spanish protectorates and Tangier International Zone. Part of Spanish Sahara added in 1958
7	Sudan	1956. Former Anglo-Egyptian condominium
8	Tunisia	1956. Former French protectorate
9	Ghana	1957. Former British colony of Gold Coast and trust territory of Togoland
10	Guinea	1958. Former part of French West Africa

Independent in 1960

11	Cameroon	Former French trust territory. Southern part of British trust territory added in 1961
12	Central African Republic	Formerly Ubangi-Chari, French Equatorial Africa
13	Chad	Former part of French Equatorial Africa
14	Congo Republic	Formerly Middle Congo, French Equatorial Africa
15	Republic of the Congo	Former Belgian colony
16	Dahomey	Former part of French West Africa
17	Gabon	Former part of French Equatorial Africa
18	Ivory Coast	Former part of French West Africa
19	Malagasy Republic	Formerly Madagascar, French overseas territory
20	Mali	Formerly French Sudan, French West Africa
21	Mauritania	Former part of French West Africa
22	Niger	Former part of French West Africa
23	Nigeria	Former British colony. Northern part of British Cameroons, trust territory, added in 1961
24	Senegal	Former part of French West Africa
25	Somali Republic	Former Italian trust territory and British protectorate of Somaliland
26	Togo	Former French trust territory of Togoland
27	Upper Volta	Former part of French West Africa

Independent after 1960

28	Sierra Leone	1961. Former British colony
29	Tanganyika	1961. Former British trust territory
30	Algeria	1962. Former French government general
31	Burundi	1962. Former part of Ruanda-Urundi, Belgian trust territory
32	Rwanda	1962. Former part of Ruanda-Urundi, Belgian trust territory
33	Uganda	1962. Former British protectorate
34	Kenya	1963. Former British colony
35	Zanzibar	1963. Former British protectorate

Dependent Territories

36	Basutoland	British colony
37	Bechuanaland	British protectorate
38	Gambia	British colony
39	Northern Rhodesia	British protectorate
40	Nyasaland	British protectorate
41	Southern Rhodesia	British colony
42	Swaziland	British protectorate
43	Comoro Islands	French overseas territory
44	French Somaliland	Overseas territory
45	Angola	Portuguese overseas province. Includes Cabinda
46	Mozambique	Portuguese overseas province
47	Portuguese Guinea	Overseas province
48	São Tomé and Principe	Portuguese overseas province
49	Canary Islands	Two Spanish metropolitan provinces
50	Ceuta and Melilla	Parts of metropolitan Spain
51	Ifni	Spanish African province
52	Spanish Guinea	African province. Includes Río Muni and Fernando Po
53	Spanish Sahara	African province

ly about the alienation of their land to Westerners. In the countries embraced by the high plateau which stretches from Kenya southward to the foot of the continent, the climate attracted white settlers in considerable numbers, and colonial administrations set aside large areas of land for them. In the Republic of South Africa 89 percent of the land is reserved to the whites. Much of this is poor, semiarid land; nevertheless, on a per capita basis more good land is reserved for the whites than for the non-whites. In Southern Rhodesia the percentage is 49. Though the percentage was much less in other dependencies–9 in the Belgian Congo, 7 in Kenya, 5 in Nyasaland, Gold Coast, and South-West Africa, and 3 in Northern Rhodesia–the grievance was keenly felt for the reason that the acreage per person was much greater for the Europeans than for the Africans. Restitution of land is a battle cry of African nationalism. One strongly stated view is that reservation of land for whites, in many instances more than they can use, has for its purpose the formation of a supply of cheap labor. A stable peasantry would dry up this reservoir of labor, but by land control, forced labor, and taxation the African peasants are driven to seek wage labor.[4]

[4] Jack Woddis, *Africa: The Roots of Revolt* (London, 1960; New York, 1962) p. 2.

Nearly all of the colonial powers in Africa were democracies; hence in many ways the colonial officials and white traders and businessmen introduced democratic ideas, if few democratic practices, into the African society. In the dependencies of central and southern Africa the governments came to be controlled by the white minority. Thus democracy was enjoyed by the whites and denied to the blacks. Indeed, the introduction of democracy into these countries was a misfortune for the Africans, for the white-dominated governments promoted the interests of the whites, much of the time at the expense of the interests of the blacks. Democratic government among a small white minority in a world of disenfranchised blacks was an anomaly and created an explosive situation. If democratic principles have validity, they have it regardless of race.

The newly independent African states have, on the one hand, to overcome the lack of unity caused by tribalism, and on the other hand, to guard against extremist nationalism. These are contradictory forces; yet their simultaneous presence is not so strange. Nationalism has developed before tribalism has disappeared, and young nationalism has a tendency to be strident. Some of the African states exhibit an aggressive nationalism even while tribalism threatens their national unity.

TWENTY-FOUR

"Nationalism is the hope and at the same time the despair of Africa," declared a study mission of United States senators who visited Africa in 1961. The senators elaborated on this conclusion as follows: "The bundle of emotions and motivations that are encompassed by the word 'nationalism' can provide tremendous driving force within a new nation. Given a point of focus, nationalism can overcome great odds. The problem is to determine this 'point of focus.' If nationalism focuses on racism it can lead to one result; if it focuses on economic development it can lead to another. If it becomes personified in worship of an individual, it may lead to political persecution; if nationalism means self-determination, it may within limits, lead toward an enlarged area of political freedom—but uncontrolled self-determination may balkanize the continent. If nationalism focuses exclusively on African problems as is natural, if it means neutrality—a plague on both your houses—an unwillingness to apply moral judgments to cold war issues, the potential impact of African nations on the world is lessened."[5]

In Europe, nationalism largely determined the size and shape of the territories of the states. In Africa,

[5]United States Senate, Committee on Foreign Relations, *Study Mission to Africa, September/October 1961,* report of Senators Albert Gore, Philip A. Hart, and Maurine B. Neuberger, January 14, 1962 (Washington, 1962).

national boundaries are almost wholly the result of the conflicts and accommodations of the imperial powers. Until the rise of nationalism in the various dependencies, the only common tie was that of alien control. The complaint is frequently made that the map of Africa was drawn by European governments without rhyme or reason. Now Africans have the determination of their national boundaries in their own control, but the result to date is an increase rather than a decrease of political entities.

Logic surely was on the side of making French Equatorial Africa and French West Africa into single sizable political units; instead they have divided into a number of small, weak states. Attempts to form larger political entities have been abortive or short-lived. Opposition to federation or union may spring from various and diverse motives. Political leaders may prefer to be sure of being top men in a smaller state than to take the chance of becoming second-rank men in larger ones; a people may fear becoming a minority in a larger population–a sentiment which may border on tribalism; or the obstacle may be the unwillingness of a territory to share its wealth with other territories not so well off in resources. The Federation of Rhodesia and Nyasaland is being dissolved into its three component parts. Nyasaland, which has an area of about 45,000 square miles and a population in the neighborhood of three million and is poor in natural resources, stood to gain much from federation with the two stronger Rhodesian territories; it nevertheless was insistent on the breakup of the federation. In the case of Katanga, on the other hand, a mineral-rich province demanded a looser political relationship with the other parts of the Republic of the Congo because it wanted to keep its ampler tax revenues at home. It felt no obligation to "subsidize" the poorer provinces of the country.

Nationalism in Africa is sometimes little removed from tribalism. Where this is the case, balkanization may well occur. Africans can ill afford to forgo the political and economic benefits which can come from integration into larger political units, especially in view of their ardent desire for modernization, but the appeal of nationalism is very persuasive. This is likewise evident in Europe. In spite of the military pressure from Russia and the demonstrated economic gains from economic integration, sophisticated Western Europeans are still reluctant to accept restrictions on their national independence of action. In Africa the fever of nationalism will most probably also have to run its course before political integration can make progress.

In east Africa a movement toward integration may be in progress, however slowly. It had its beginning in colonial days. In 1900 the East Africa (Kenya) and Uganda protectorates amalgamated their postal services and as one system became a member of the Universal Postal Union. In 1917 the two territories were united in a customs union, and in 1927 Tanganyika was incorporated in it. A further step was taken on January 1, 1948, when the High Commission for East Africa was established by the British government. A number of interterritorial concerns were placed under its care, among them Makerere College, aviation, transport, and communications, customs, and research and science. In 1961 the High Commission was reorganized and became the East African Common Services Organization. A Central Legislative Assembly controls the functions and policies of the organization. Prime Ministers Jomo Kenyatta of Kenya, Milton Obote of Uganda, and President Julius Nyerere of Tanganyika are exploring the possibilities of a closer political and economic federation of their territories.[6]

Political cooperation on a continental scale—pan-African-ism—had its beginning among what may be called Overseas Negroes, when few Negroes in Africa were articulate. The first Pan-African Congress met in London in 1900. Its sponsor was H. Sylvester Williams, a West Indies

[6]Carl G. Rosberg and Aaron Segal, "An East African Federation," *International Conciliation*, May, 1963; New York *Times*, June 4, 1963.

barrister. At this congress Dr. William E. Burghardt du Bois, an American Negro of mixed blood, uttered the prophetic words: "The problem of the twentieth century is the problem of the color line–the relation of the darker to the lighter races of men in Asia and Africa, in America and the islands of the sea."[7] Du Bois was for several decades a leader in the pan-African movement. Marcus Aurelius Garvey, a West Indian, was his chief rival for leadership. Subsequent Pan-African congresses were held in 1919 (Paris), 1921 (London and Brussels), 1923 (London and Lisbon), 1927 (New York), and 1945 (Manchester).

With the rise of independent states in Africa the movement was bound to become centered in that continent. In 1958 the First Conference of Independent African States met in Accra, Ghana. All of the African states which were independent at the time were present, with the exception of South Africa, but of the eight only Ghana and Liberia belonged to Black Africa. Five were predominantly Arab and Moslem, while the eighth, Ethiopia, belonged to neither group. In a declaration adopted by the conference the members asserted and proclaimed "unity among ourselves and our solidarity with the dependent peoples of Africa" and resolved to "preserve among ourselves the fundamen-

[7]Colin Legum, *Pan Africanism: A Short Political Guide* (New York, 1962).

tal unity of outlook on foreign policy so that a distinctive African personality will play its part in co-operation with other peace-loving nations to further the cause of Peace." In a series of resolutions the conference declared "the existence of colonialism in any form or shape" to be a "threat to the security and independence of the African States and to world peace" and demanded that "rapid steps" be taken toward self-determination and independence, recognized the right of the Algerian people to independence and affirmed its "determination to make every possible effort" to help the Algerian people to attain independence, called for the development of cultural cooperation among African states, and expressed views in favor of a foreign policy of neutralism and nonalignment.

That the first conference of African states met at Accra was no accident, for Kwame Nkrumah, the president of Ghana, is the most eloquent and insistent advocate of pan-Africanism and the projection of the "African personality" in world affairs. He is stongly of the view that Africa must unite or perish. He seems to think that the former French colonies which are members of the French Community have only a fictitious independence, that the former colonial powers are engineering division and "seeking to make Africa a warground for contending interests," and that "it is only in the African association of unity and not in a rider-horse relationship with the very powers that are planning our balkanization that we can counteract and surmount this machiavellian danger." He considers "that even the idea of regional federations in Africa is fraught with many dangers." President Nkrumah sums up the advantages of pan-Africanism as follows: "A union of African states must strengthen our influence on the international scene, as all Africa will speak with one concerted voice. With union, our example of a multiple of peoples living and working for mutual development in amity and peace will point the way for the smashing of the inter-territorial barriers existing elsewhere, and give a new meaning to the concept of human brotherhood. A Union of African States will raise the dignity of Africa and strengthen its impact on world affairs. It will make possible the full expression of the African personality."[8]

It is not always clear what Nkrumah means by "union." The Ghana-Guinea union of 1959 was envisaged as the inauguration of a Union of Independent African States, for that is the title used in the declaration issued at the time. Membership was open to all independent African states or federations. However, "Each State or Federation which is a member of the Union shall preserve its own individuality and structure" (Art. 2), and "The States or

[8]*Africa Must Unite* (London, 1960), p. 193.

THIRTY-ONE

Federations shall have their own foreign representatives" (Art. 7). The charter of the short-lived Ghana-Guinea-Mali union of 1960 contained the same provisions. The term "union" as it is used here means no more than a political alliance. However, in his book, *Africa Must Unite*, Nkrumah pleads for a stronger union—one which will have the exclusive powers of overall economic planning, defense, and foreign relations.[9]

Pan-Africanism faces many obstacles. The deep divisions in Africa have already been noted. Politically the outlook of the thirty-four independent states is far from uniform. Egypt is seeking to amalgamate with two non-African countries; the six northern African states are members of the Arab League. Twelve former French colonies (popularly known as the Brazzaville group) are members of the French Community and associate members of the European Economic Community and have united in an Afro-Malagasy Union for cooperation in defense, economics, and foreign policy. Five former British colonies are members of the Commonwealth. Nineteen states, including the Brazzaville group, belong to the so-called Monrovia powers, a relatively moderate group which is willing to accept the cooperation of Western countries in developing Africa; and six states are members of the

[9] *Ibid.*, chap. 21, "Continental Government for Africa."

THIRTY-TWO

Casablanca group which is aggressively neutralist. While there is some overlapping of memberships, each of these groups has a distinct orientation.

There are causes of dissension. The northern Arab, Moslem countries, and especially Egypt, want all African states to boycott Israel. The Casablanca Conference branded the latter as an "instrument in the service of imperialism and neo-colonialism." But Israel has developed excellent relations with the west African countries. It is giving the countries of tropical Africa valuable technical assistance, and more than 2,000 Africans were brought to Israel in 1962 for training. Ethiopia has recently given *de jure* recognition to Israel and the two countries are about to exchange ambassadors. Nasser has declared the economic and cultural "infiltration" of the continent by Israel to be a serious problem for the Arab countries, but in the interests of African unity he is not pressing the issue on the other African states.

While imperialism caused tensions between Western powers, it also hid or suppressed clashes of interests of the various peoples of Africa. These are now causing tensions between the new independent states. For example, Morocco claims sovereignty over Mauretania, and the Somali Republic demands the cession of the northern half of Kenya and a large section of Ethiopia on the ground that a majority of the inhabitants of these areas are Somali. Morocco and Algeria have spilled blood. Nasser of Egypt aspires to head a pan-Arab union.

One of the chief obstacles to pan-Africanism seems to be President Nkrumah himself. Many suspect that his ardent advocacy of African unity is inspired by personal ambition. The late president of Togo, with whom Nkrumah carried on a bitter feud, called the latter "a black imperialist."

Leadership of the pan-African movement was taken over by Emperor Haile Selassie of Ethiopia when he called a conference of the heads of African states at Addis Ababa in May, 1963. Thirty governments were represented. President Nkrumah pleaded fervently for a federation along the lines of the United States. "We must unite now or perish," he declared, "since no single African state is large or powerful enough to stand on its own against unbridled imperialist exploitation of her men and resources and the growing complexities of the modern world." He opposed separate political or economic groupings on the ground that they tend "to scatter energy resources and promote interstate rivalries and disputes."[10]

Nkrumah's plan received little support. It was regarded as going "too far and too fast." It was felt that African

[10]New York *Times,* May 20, 1963.

unity had to be built "brick by brick." Emperor Haile Selassie pleaded for a moderate course. "Tradition cannot be abandoned at once," he declared, "but we shirk our responsibilities to Africa and the Africans we lead unless we begin working for the future." He argued that a federation like that advocated by Nkrumah was impractical, as the widely divergent states would not agree to it and disagreement would delay and impede progress. He proposed a plan modeled after the Organization of American States. He also pleaded for moderation of African attitudes toward the former colonial powers. Africa needs help, he declared, and should conduct its international relations "devoid of resentment and hostilities."[11]

The conference accepted the emperor's views in general. A charter was adopted establishing an Organization of African Unity. It provides for an annual assembly of heads of state and government with power to adopt resolutions by a two-thirds majority. A Council of Ministers with similar powers will meet twice a year. Neither can make binding decisions. The charter also provides for a secretariat, headed by a secretary general, and a Commission on Mediation and Conciliation to settle disputes.[12] The charter calls for cooperation in the fields of economics, culture, education, and transport and communication. The

[11] *Ibid.*, May 23, 1963.
[12] *Ibid.*, May 26, 1963.

headquarters of the organization temporarily will be in Addis Ababa.

The conference also adopted a number of important resolutions. One called for an all-out effort to rid Africa of colonialism and white domination. Members were called upon to deny airspace and landing facilities to South African planes, and a nine-nation committee was set up to plan active aid for nationalist guerrillas. It is difficult to escape the impression that the spirit of unity which prevailed at the conference has its origin in the bitter resentment of all Africans against the continued colonialism in Angola and Mozambique and the white supremacy governments of Southern Rhodesia and South Africa.

Pan-Africanism is unlikely to have any widespread popular support, however, until some fundamental economic problems have been answered. The annual per capita incomes of the countries of sub-Sahara Africa, with the exception of the Republic of South Africa, are among the lowest in the world. The question has been raised as to whether the resources of Africa are adequate to support a better economy. While its natural resources are considerable, they must not be exaggerated. Africa is a large continent, but deserts occupy about one-fourth of its total area and semiarid regions are extensive. In the latter the dry season lasts from eight to nine months

and the rainy season is highly irregular. The soil generally is infertile and subject to erosion. Agriculture is further
handicapped by a capricious climate. Droughts and co-
pious rains follow no set pattern. Except in a few areas the
agricultural base is insufficient to support the apparatus and
services of a modern state, to say nothing of insuring a
high level of living.

The mineral resources of Africa are by no means mea-
ger, and the full extent of them is not yet known. Besides
the precious metals for which South Africa is famous,
sub-Sahara Africa has rich deposits of iron ore, copper,
tin, cobalt, chrome ore, manganese ore, and considerable
amounts of radioactive ores. However, these deposits are
unevenly distributed. As far as is now known, tropical
Africa is poorly endowed with coal and petroleum. Africa,
however, possesses an estimated 40 percent of the world's
potential hydroelectric power.

In spite of a fair endowment in natural resources[13] the
outlook for economic development in the foreseeable future
is rather discouraging. Eugene R. Black, former president
of the World Bank, has characterized the encounter be-

[13]Some African specialists hold that the continent is richly endowed. One
writes that "the continent of Africa is rich and potentially much richer still.
It is indeed not the presence or absence of natural wealth which is responsible
for the poverty of the African people, but the system under which Africans have
been compelled to live and the use to which their wealth has been put by the
Western Powers who have ruled Africa for so long." Woddis, p. 214.

tween Africa and the West as "a meeting between two ages of time. The life of most of the continent's 250 million peoples is in some respects less advanced than Europe's in the Dark Ages. Particularly in the tropical zone Africa's lands and peoples are a mosaic of many small pieces, largely without even the unifying influence of common language, common religion or shared historical experience. So, while superstition, ignorance, disease and poverty are widespread, it is hard to mount a sweeping attack against them, so crisscrossed and divided is Africa by national boundaries, natural barriers and cultural differences. And so different are both the natural and the cultural settings of Africa that the technology and social institutions of Europe will not necessarily provide easily workable models for the Africa of tomorrow."[14]

Black probably speaks with the caution of a banker who is discussing a loan with a prospective borrower, but the views of Dr. George T. Kimble, a leading authority on Africa and the director of a broad and intensive survey of tropical Africa, are very similar. In his judgment only six of the twenty-six newly independent states of Africa have a chance of surviving as "truly autonomous, virile and stable members of the family of nations." The twenty others he fears "are doomed to weakness and suffering, to

[14]In an address at The Hague, Netherlands, October 29, 1962.

THIRTY-EIGHT

a life at best, of stint and scheming; at worst, of impotence and indebtedness."[15]

Something has already been said about colonialism as a diffuser of Western values, attitudes, and advances in education, science, and administration. That colonialism served this function can be seen from a comparison of conditions in Ethiopia and Liberia with those in the one-time dependencies. Ethiopia, which is the oldest independent country in Africa, and in the world, is in some ways the most backward country in Africa, and Liberia, which has never been subject to foreign rule and which has been an independent state since 1847, has serious deficiencies and lags in its social, political, and educational fields. Liberians are aware of the fact that colonial status need not necessarily be all disadvantageous. While they are proud of their long history of independence, they "always miss and often tend to resent the scarcity of the basic developmental facilities which most colonial countries have given their dependencies."[16]

Ethiopia demonstrates to a marked degree that political

[15]New York *Times,* December 7, 1962. A contrary view is that of Chester Bowles, who holds that "on balance Africa's present development and long-term future prospects appear remarkably promising." *Ibid.,* June 16, 1963 (magazine section).

[16]United States Senate, Committee on Foreign Relations, *Study Mission to Africa,* November-December 1960, report of Senators Frank Church, Gale W. McGee, and Frank E. Moss, February 12, 1961 (Washington, 1961), p. 35.

independence is no guarantee of progress or freedom. A committee of United States senators who constituted a study mission to Africa in 1960 declared that "Ethiopia could be viewed as a close approximation to a kingdom of the European Middle Ages. Power and the best land are held by the virtually absolute monarch, the intensely conservative Ethiopian Coptic Christian Church, and the great nobles of the provinces; a tenant-farming peasantry is sustained by a fertile land cultivated by the most primitive methods." The Committee concluded that there appears "almost no chance for any but the slowest and most long-range successes in the basic fields of economic development in Ethiopia."[17]

Africa is receiving large amounts in foreign economic aid. In 1960 it received $1,400,000,000, which was 37 percent of the total of grants and loans extended to underdeveloped countries in that year. France was first among the donors, with $732,000,000; the United States second, for a total of $231,000,000; Britain third with $144,000,000; and Belgium fourth with $86,000,000. Communist countries in 1960 allocated an estimated $963,000,000 in foreign aid to African countries. On a per capita basis African countries received about twice as much as underdeveloped countries generally.[18]

[17]*Ibid.*, pp. 14, 16.
[18]New York *Times,* March 4, 1962.

FORTY

Foreign aid is important, but unless it can operate in a favorable environment, its effectiveness will not be great. Robert L. Garner, who served for nine years as vice president of the International Bank for Reconstruction and Development and five years as president of the International Finance Corporation, concludes "economic development or lack of it is primarily due to difference in their political, social and religious institutions." Too great a reliance on foreign aid could have insidious consequences. In many countries it was used as an excuse for failure to mobilize the nation's resources and to insure that "internal conditions which hinder development are improved." According to Garner, the more important prerequisites of economic advancement are: consistent law and order, an honest and effective public administration, financial stability (an absence of severe inflation), a "sensible" plan of development, an honest and effective tax system, and a society in which wealth and power are not in the hands of a few.[19]

Nearly all African countries under the colonial regimes rated fairly well with respect to these prerequisites. Whether the new, inexperienced governments can maintain and improve their rating is the real test. In any case the task of raising economic standards in Africa is extremely difficult.

[19]*Ibid.*, September 22, 1962.

The United Nations Economic Commission for Africa has estimated that to raise the standards of consumption to the level prevailing in Western industrialized countries in 1960 would require the doubling of agricultural and a 25-fold increase in industrial output. At an annual rate of increase of 7 to 8 percent in industry and 1 to 2 percent in agriculture, it would take 40 to 50 years to attain this level.

Economic and political developments will strongly influence each other. In the movement for political independence, expectations of higher living levels were aroused. Economic improvement lags and tax revenues fall far behind expenditures with resultant financial and political difficulties for the new governments. The democratic governments with which the new states begin their national independence come under increasing pressure. A few already have fallen to coups by the military or dictatorships.

For centuries Africa played a passive role in the world; it has now become an active force, and the change has occurred within a decade. This continental shift from powerlessness to critical importance must be counted among the great revolutions of our times. Africa, though economically and militarily weak, enjoys great power in world politics. Neither the West nor the Communist bloc can afford to see the African states move into the orbit of the other; each would like to have their good will, if they cannot win their active support. African states are benefiting from, if not exploiting, this rivalry.

The United Nations is the chief instrument of the great influence which Africa wields in world politics. The continent has a membership of thirty-four, excluding South Africa, in the world organization. Within the next year or two this number will be increased by at least three. Thus the African states constitute nearly a third of the total membership of the United Nations. For passage in the General Assembly important measures require a two-thirds majority; hence the African states alone nearly command a veto in that important organ, provided they stand united. Because of the rule giving each member one vote, regardless of population or financial contribution, Gabon, with less than half a million people, has an equal vote with the United States, with a population of 190,000,000, or India with about 450,000,000. That these African states with a combined population not much larger than that of the United States should have 32 times more votes may be an anomaly, but it is an important fact in current world politics. It produces a strange paradox. Overwhelming military power is concentrated in two states, Russia and the United States, but because of the United Nations, political power is widely diffused.

The importance of the United Nations for the small

states in general and the African states in particular is obvious. They cannot afford to allow the United Nations to become weakened. Yet it was the situation in the Congo which put a severe strain on the United Nations, financially and otherwise. Should similar situations develop in Angola and Mozambique, the United Nations might well be burdened beyond its capacity. Yet it is in this direction that the fierce hatred of colonialism is driving the African states. Another ominous move was the walkout staged in the conference of the International Labor Organization which met in Geneva in June, 1963, as a protest against the presence of delegates from South Africa. Since there is no provision for the expulsion of a member of the I.L.O., the thirty-two African members resorted to this method to force South Africa out of the organization. The bitterness of Africans against the white-minority-dominated government of South Africa and its policy of extreme racial discrimination is understandable, but if the African states boycott the General Assembly of the United Nations and the Conferences of the Specialized Agencies, they will undermine the very institution which has been their protector and the source of their great political power.

The African members of the United Nations may also be establishing precedents of intervention in the internal affairs of member states which may conceivably be turned against them. If white minority domination in Southern Rhodesia and South Africa is a concern of the United Nations, why not dictatorial rule or feudalism in African countries? Some African states are anything but models of liberalism and democracy. Some of their leaders practice authoritarianism at home but fight colonialism abroad. They all make much of the evils of colonialism, of the damage it does to the human spirit, yet Haile Selassie, who as emperor is the near-absolute ruler of a country which is extremely backward politically, economically, and socially, emerged from the 1963 Addis Ababa conference as the hero of African nationalism and unity. The evils of colonialism and dictatorship are essentially the same, but at this stage Africans are more interested in national than individual or personal freedom. It is hoped that this will change when their national independence is assured and they acquire more maturity.

It is widely believed in the United States that African neutralism in the United Nations has leaned heavily in favor of the Communist bloc. The fact that both the African and Communist members of the United Nations have fought colonialism, though for different reasons, has made it appear so. As a matter of fact the African states have shown a marked independence in their voting on issues before the General Assembly. Africans are Africa-centered, which under the circumstances is what might be expected.

The West has not always been wise in its dealings with Africa, but neither has Russia and the other Communist countries. Both Guinea and Ghana seem to be disillusioned with Communist promises and performances. There are indications that Ghana is turning to the right and desires to attract the investment of private foreign capital, for Russian aid and goods have fallen much below expectations. In April, 1963, it published a new law which embodies the principle that nationalization will occur only in exceptional circumstances, and that if it does take place, there will be fair compensation, the amount to be determined by an outside arbitrator if necessary. Reports of racial discimination against African students in Moscow and in satellite countries is an embarrassing development and no aid to Communist propaganda. The current controversy between China and Russia with respect to the true, pure Communist ideology and world strategy also has its repercussions in Africa.

There is time still, then, for the West, and particularly the United States, to work with the African nations in building for the future. How best this can be done, Professor Brookes discusses in the next chapter.

TWO

THE topic of the City of God and the City of Man in Africa which is so appropriate to our own times began some fifteen and a half centuries ago in North Africa. It is good for us to span the years and to see our contemporary problems and opportunities in the light of that thought which closed the classicial era of Rome and opened the Middle Ages.

In the year 410, Rome, which had not been entered by any foreign enemy for more than seven centuries, was sacked by the Goths. The majestic and unconquerable city now shared the fate of the ordinary cities of the world. The significance of the event was as great as if Hitler had made a triumphal march through London, or if the Japanese navy had landed troops to occupy Washington. It was the end of an era, the downfall of the secure and accepted things on which not merely civilised life but ordered Christianity had been built. Three years later, St. Augustine began to write his magnificent book, *De Civitate Dei* (The City of God). It took him thirteen years to write. Four years after he had finished it, he died in his episcopal city of Hippo, straitly besieged by the Vandals, with no ray of earthly hope to cheer him. But because he believed in the City of God, he died in peace and he died victorious.

The man who wrote this book was a North African, and at the same time a Roman citizen. It is improbable that he was, as has been represented by some modern writers, a black man, but he would certainly have had trouble under the *apartheid* laws if he had lived in the Republic of South Africa. He was sufficiently an African to make his life and work germane to the present condition of Africa. He was also a Roman citizen, proud of his citizenship and writing his books in the universal language of Rome. Much more important in his eyes-and surely in ours too-he was a Christian, with his ultimate patriotism fixed in Heaven, his ultimate loyalty given to that City which hath foundations whose builder and maker is God. To him loyalty to the City of God was the supreme loyalty which incorporated and transcended all other loyalties. To it he gave the absolute allegiance of his mind and spirit. It is not enough to say that this loyalty came first. Other loyalties only existed at all for him in so far as they might be incorporated with it or taken up into it. This grand conception is vital to an understanding not only of St. Augustine's day but ours. It meets our problems, and if we would accept it, it answers them. In my recent book, I have tried to apply his message to our times.[1] I shall here try to carry it further in the light of what we have seen of the new Africa during recent years.

St. Augustine defines the City of God as the city of those who love God to the contempt of self, and the City of Man as the city of those who love self to the contempt of God. These two conceptions are irreconcilably different, and we cannot reduce them to any sort of unity. In the world of ultimate truth they remain forever apart and distinct, the one conception the perpetual enemy of the other. But as St. Augustine himself says, they are so "intertwined and intermixed" in "the course of these declining times" that we never find either of them in complete purity

---

[1] *The City of God and the Politics of Crisis* (Oxford, 1960).

on earth. This is to say, in other words, that we can never really separate Dr. Jekyll and Mr. Hyde in our personality, irreconcilable enemies though they be. Only one Man has ever walked this earth without sin. I suppose that no one of us has ever met, on the other hand, any fellow human being who is utterly evil without any spark of goodness in him. As we look at ourselves or, if we find that process too painful, if we look at our friends, we see the strange intermixture of good and bad. We see it in our nation; we see it in every political organization. Though there is much that is evil in the State, we never find any State which is wholly bad. Law, which is only fulfilled in love, has none the less its own virtue, its own autonomous place in the Commonwealth of God. And on the other hand the Christian Church, although it is the best that men have ever been able to do to institutionalize the City of God among men, is itself a very mixed body. Even Augustine, orthodox bishop of the Catholic Church though he was, speaks both of those within the Church who are not of the City of God and of those without the Church who do in fact belong to the Heavenly City.

So we face this strange "intertwined and intermixed" condition of all human society. The acceptance of this fact does not hinder us from accepting the magnificent conception of the City of God, nor from distinguishing with true clarity between it and that City of Man which struggles with it for our all allegiance.

From most of North Africa the Christian faith and the Christian Church was swept away by the victorious achievement of Islam. The subject Copts in Egypt and an isolated island of Christianity in Ethiopia alone remained to continue the tradition of the Church of North Africa in which St. Augustine lived. The contact of Christianity with Africa as we know it comes mainly from the sixteenth and, on a large scale, from the nineteenth centuries, when Western Europe and America brought the Gospel to the peoples of the African continent. The coming of the missionaries was in a very real sense the bringing back of the City of God to the people of Africa. They needed it. Let us not fall into the trap into which so many have fallen of taking the African and the Asian as they are after generations of missionary work, or of painting an idealised and misleading picture of primitive Africa and coming to the conclusion that missionary work was not necessary, though there undoubtedly were great African virtues–discipline, order, obedience to authority, respect for law, respect for elders, hospitality, and a joy in life. Early missionaries very often lacked humility in that they were unwilling to learn, though ready to teach, and they sometimes did scant justice to the virtues which they found. These were mixed with lust and cruelty and, far the most terrible of all, with an all-pervailing fear of evil spiritual forces. We need not apologise for the missions or for missionary work. What has happened in Africa today has only been possible because of it. Even where missionaries have been repudiated by freedom movements, they have in fact in history been the source and inspiration of these movements.

We may then rightly think of the missionaries as those who were used to bring to Africa the City of God. Let us look at them for a moment. Perhaps the most famous of them all, David Livingstone, might be taken as an example. We must grant without hesitation that there were moments when the explorer and the geographer seemed to dominate the missionary, but there can be no doubt of Livingstone's internal source of power or of his caring for Africans. The man who could sing (in the original Latin) as he tramped around Africa,

> Dulcis Iesu memoria,
> Dans nobis vera gaudia,
> Sed super mel et omnia
> Eius dulcis presentia.
>
> (Jesus, the very thought of Thee
> With sweetness fills my breast;

FIFTY-TWO

But sweeter far Thy face to see,
And in Thy presence rest.)

cannot be regarded as an unspiritual ecclesiastical statesman. There was something mystic in the religion of this
man, so strangely descended, having one grandfather who
was a minister of the Auld Secession Kirk and the other
grandfather who was out with Prince Charlie in the heather.
But, devout Christian though he was, David Livingstone
held very strongly that it was to the advantage of Africa
for Britain to annex large portions of it, for only so would
the slave trade be overcome and would trade and commerce
in general be encouraged in Africa. It does not follow
that Livingstone was wrong there. Annexation might be
right in 1863 and disannexation in 1963. Still, Livingstone, one of the most intrepid and heroic of missionaries, must be linked up with what after ages have been
pleased to call imperialism.

Let us take another example: those pioneer missionaries of the American Board of Missions who landed in
my own Province of Natal in the Republic of South Africa
one hundred and twenty-seven years ago. Look particularly
at two of them–Newton Adams and Daniel Lindley. Newton
Adams was a qualified doctor. He spent his life attending
the sick among the Zulu people and preaching the Gospel.
Incidentally he waited eleven years for his first convert,

but never gave up. Before his early death he had ministered not only to the Zulus, but to the emigrant Boers or Voortrekkers, and to the British garrison, being the joint medical officer to those two opposing forces. He, the most missionary-hearted of men, who had come to Africa to give himself to the Africans in complete humility and sacrifice, nevertheless found himself bound up with the needs of the white settlers and the white garrison.

Still more clearly was this the case with Daniel Lindley, an ardent Presbyterian minister from Virginia. He too came ready to give his whole heart to the Africans of Natal. The time came when the emigrant Voortrekkers arrived in Natal with no ordained minister and in deep spiritual need. Lindley became the *predikant* or minister of these his fellow Presbyterians, whose language he learned. His "parish" included the whole Province of Natal and portions of the Transvaal and of the Orange Free State. Thirty years ago there were still living in South Africa old people whose parents he had married and whom he had baptised or received into Church membership. Most strikingly, it was this American missionary who received Paul Kruger into Church membership–that Paul Kruger in whose name and according to whose traditions the present policy of *apartheid* in the Republic of South Africa has been conceived. When in the end a minister of the Dutch Reformed Church came up from the Cape Colony to minister to the emigrant farmers, Lindley, who had preached the first Dutch and the first English sermons in my own city of Pietermaritzburg, went back quietly and happily to his first call and spent the rest of a long and useful life in ministering to the Zulus.

There were men whose single-heartedness in the missionary endeavour none can doubt, but who were inevitably and inextricably mixed up as friends and benefactors of the white settlers. Could they have done otherwise? Would they have been greater or smaller men of God if they had withheld their love from the white men around them? And yet there can be no doubt that the association of missionaries in one way or another with the colonising powers, with the garrisons and with the settlers, has made it more difficult for them to maintain themselves in the condition of emergent African nationalism. Protestant missionaries have had a more difficult task in this respect than Catholics, because they were mostly married men who had children born on the mission field. Let no one think that this was a pity. The epic of the missionary wife in Africa still has to be written. It contains some of the surest, strongest, and tenderest examples of Christian heroism in history. Nevertheless the position of the missionaries' children was an equivocal one. In countries where there were white settlers it could not be otherwise than that the children of the missionaries should mingle with the children of the settlers. These were the most natural contacts. If the missionaries' children were to have schooling, they would have to go to the schools built for the children of white settlers. Inevitably even those of them who shared their fathers' dedication to the welfare of the African and who showed it through long lives of service became, they and their children after them, integrated to an increasing extent with the white population. One of the most outstanding supporters of *apartheid* in the Republic of South Africa is descended from a French Protestant missionary, who could never have conceived that any descendant of his would have taken such a position.

The point that I would make here in a preliminary way – I shall come back to it later – is that this is the only way in which the faith of Christ could have been brought to Africa, that those things which are sometimes brought up as articles of charge against missionaries and against Christianity are part of that strange mixed thing which we call life, which Jesus Christ our Lord was content to share with us.

The coming of the missionaries brought to Africa faith, love, self-sacrifice, and magnificent examples of Christian living. They brought, as Christianity has always brought, new freedom to women and little children. They brought also wisdom, technical ability, scholastic knowledge, and science. All these are of God. It is the most dangerous heresy to suggest that they come from any other source. If one looks at the city of Johannesburg, for example, one will see all of these things. There is faith and love to be found there. It is often a very generous city. Its towering buildings rising up to the skies and its mines sinking in some cases as low as a mile below the surface of the earth are all part of that civilisation with which the wisdom and the knowledge of God is mixed. But who could, without exposing himself to well-merited ridicule, point to Johannesburg as an example of the City of God? The City of Gold, yes, but hardly the City of God. Beside its towering skyscrapers and above its fantastically deep mines are the sordid and squalid dwelling places of thousands of people on whose poverty much of the superficial wealth is built. It is a city where vice flourishes as well as generosity, where disease, hunger, and infantile mortality are to be found side by side with culture and luxurious living. It is a strangely mixed city. The City of Man at its worst is "intermixed and intertwined" with the City of God.

Let us take as another illustration a city which has grown up on the place where Adams and Lindley landed, the city of Durban. It is a city of great scenic beauty, of exotic sub-tropical appeal. But one only has to make a careful tour of it to see how the white people have kept for themselves the cooler areas, with good views and with the sea breeze, and left for the Indians and Africans the hotter, flatter parts of the town with no view. As one travels down from the Berea, the hill overlooking the Port of Durban, one comes at the bottom of the slopes to the areas into which the Indians have begun to move since the white people have begun to give them up, and this move has been called Indian penetration and has been the subject of restrictive legislation.

Behind the Berea is a sun-baked area with no sea breeze and no view called Cato Manor. In it until recently 80,000 Africans and a few Indians lived in conditions of unutterable squalor. Under the Group Areas legislation of the Republic of South Africa, it has been proclaimed as a white area. When I last saw it, there were still some 30,000 Africans living there. I have had few experiences more poignant than the tour which I made through it recently with a number of university teachers of social science. There, where one could have expected sullenness, if not open hostility, was friendliness – crowds of smiling children, cheering and waving to the bus. There amid the hovels were the little buildings with the Cross on them, so that the Church of Christ had followed these people even into that hell.

Such is Durban. And yet it is also a generous city. In

Cato Manor white South Africans have worked with immense self-sacrifice to mitigate the evil caused by the system. But with the Gospel which Adams, Lindley, and so many others spread, there has become "intermixed and intertwined" exploitation, arrogance, greed, and the colour bar.

Yet so the faith of Christ came, and only so could it come, fallen man being what he is and history being what it is. As we draw the skirts of our garments aside from the evil in situations of this kind, we try to exalt our righteousness above that of Christ. The Incarnation, Christ's entry into history, was the supreme example of God's care for the world of man as it is. First-century Palestine was no paradise. It is very important for us to recognise frankly that the evil which accompanied the coming of the City of God to Africa during the last century was inevitable so long as sin remains unconquered among men. When we hear talk today of "colonialism," "imperialism," the "missionary exploiter," we must realise that whatever truth there is in these terms there is a wrong spirit at work which uses them – a spirit of anti-Christ which has become mixed up with the magnificent liberation movement of our day.

Before discussing this liberation movement and of the glory and splendour of it and of all that it should mean to us, I must refer to some of the difficulties which have accompanied the emergence of African States into their new freedom. It is one of the strangest phenomena in history that Africa, so long despised, should now have become the subject of one of the strangest auctions in history, the auction between the United States and the Soviet Union for African support. I am one of those who hold the view that it is not the Soviet Union which is exploiting Africa, but Africa which is exploiting the Soviet Union. Africa is the *tertius gaudens* in this struggle for supremacy. As the two main bidders call against one another in this almost cosmic auction, the other players–Britain, France and the rest–fall into the background. They are silent not because they are unable or unworthy, but because they are the colonising powers from whom liberation is taking place.

In the attitude of the United States towards Africa there is much genuine humanitarianism, much genuine unselfishness, much desire to help Africa for the sake of Africa. But there has also been an element of trying to beat the Soviets, an atmosphere in which Africa has been treated as a means to an end in a great game of power politics. The two conceptions which America has brought most clearly to the new Africa are those of anti-colonialism or anti-imperialism, and of "one man, one vote." These are natural gifts. In desiring freedom from imperialist rule, America is only wishing for other nations her own experience. The spirit of 1776 lives to illuminate the world of 1963. And if the United States is willing to support "one man, one vote" even where it means putting a former ruling white group under a former subject black group, we will remember that in the years after the Civil War the United States followed the same policy in its own South. In this way the United States has been responsible for indirectly encouraging African nationalism through its opposition to colonial rule and for directly encouraging constitutional liberty in the form of universal franchise. It is essentially the political philosophy of Rousseau, however unconscious. And while the Soviet Union has on the whole failed in converting the Africans to a positive programme of Marxism, it has been able to bring a negative attack, decrying the true values of the faith, which has exposed the missionaries and the Christian Church to danger and contumely, and poured scorn on some of the noblest ideals of the West. America should have had so much more to give. She has given it in men, in goodwill, and in technological skill, but not in political philosophy. To begin one's political life with the philosophy of Rousseau, tinctured and besmirched with Marxism, is a poor beginning. America should have had so much more to give.

I once asked an American professor visiting South Africa if he could give some lectures on American political philosophy. He said, "There is no such thing." He told me that Americans had traditions of which they were very proud and institutions which they valued, but that they had no real formulated philosophy of the State. In the American Constitution which gives formal body to the Law of Nature, in the American outlook which incorporates so much that is sound and wise in the teaching of that great liberal, John Locke, in the American doctrine of the separation of powers which bases itself on the work of that great Frenchman, Montesquieu, there was surely much that America could have given to Africa. She has not given it. It seems that in this great age when America has done so much, this is one field where she has largely failed.

But perhaps this is in some measure unfair, because after all the deeply held American doctrines of anti-colonialism and universal franchise have been applied in areas under British and French rule where the institutions which they were made to run were the institutions of the cabinet system. To take Ghana as a striking example, complete independence and universal franchise were superimposed upon a sovereign parliament, a completely flexible constitution, a cabinet system which could be an instrument of freedom only if there was a strong opposition, and a dynamic nationalist leader who was determined to give no opposition a chance of overthrowing his government.

These are the difficulties under which Africa enters its

new phase. But they must not be allowed to obscure for us the greatness of the liberation movement. In some ways ever since the Reformation, and certainly during the last century, the almost countless millions of Asia and Africa have been given an inferior position in the world which is their birthright and their true mother country no less than that of Britons, Americans, or South Africans. The colour-bar, growing so subtly, has deprived them of opportunities and cramped and hindered their personalities. They have been exposed not so much to cruelty or brutality, but to that which is harder to bear than either–contempt. And contempt is sometimes the worse when it is half-shown and half-paternalistic. It was time that the colour-bar should be shaken and destroyed. We can rejoice that we live in the age of this great movement. Even those of us who, as a political minority in South Africa, are exposed to the full blast of the disapproval of our fellow-countrymen can rejoice that we are living now and are able to take our part in our devastatingly difficult sector of the fighting line in this great battle.

No prudential arguments should keep us from taking up a firm and joyful stand for this new human freedom and quality. The campaign against the colour-bar which has led to the independence of the African States is just, right, timely, and indeed overdue. It may be compared with the liberation of slaves, with the years 1793 to 1833 in Great Britain, with the tremendous years 1861 to 1865 in the United States. Ministers of religion in the Deep South could justify slavery, as ministers of the Dutch Reformed Church in South Africa can justify *apartheid.* But who reads their manuscripts now, except as historical curiosities? The forces fighting against liberation might have a leader like Robert E. Lee, one of the world's greatest men–just, honest, brave, unselfish, a Christian gentleman, and an inspiration to his fellows–but by some terrible mischance fighting on the wrong side and for the wrong cause. The greatness of Abraham Lincoln lay in the fact that with all his human frailties and complexities he was able to pierce through all arguments and prejudices to the very heart of the question and to take up a firm and clear position on the right side.

The emancipation of slaves did not bring about a new heaven and a new earth. The freed slaves were neither archangels nor saints. Much had to be done before they were truly fit for citizenship. Yet emancipated they had to be, and any delay in emancipation would have been a sin.

Let us take another example, the emancipation of women, which has been one of the outstanding features of the twentieth century. No man in his senses would want to go back now to the nineteenth century with its artificialities and sentimentalities, its apparent respect for women and its real refusal of rights of human equality to them. The world is not necessarily a very much better place because they are emancipated. It does not follow that women are on the whole better than men or, for that matter, that Africans are better than Europeans. The fact is that a great urge came to humanity–and from whom could it have come except from the Holy Spirit of God? That liberation had to take place, and whether women use their freedom wisely or unwisely, they must have it. There once again was not a new world. The tactics of the woman's liberation movement were not always above reproach, with suffragettes chaining themselves to the galleries of the House of Commons so that they could interrupt the pro- ceedings, with a leading suffragette flinging herself before the King's horse during the Derby. These were not nec- essarily the best or most balanced ways of working for freedom, nor is it always the best and most balanced ways which are used today in Kenya, or Guinea or Ghana. But the day of liberation has come. It is a movement which also comes from the Spirit of God, from the Spirit of God moving on the face of the waters. It is another milestone in the great path of freedom. Accept it we must, and re- joice in it.

But we must accept it with level eyes that see that not all that happened under colonial administration was bad and that not all that is happening in the new nations is good.

SIXTY-FIVE

What we accord to them, as it seems to me, is a real love of Africa and the Africans, a love which will refuse to treat them as a mere means to an end in the great game of power politics, or even of Western self-defence. The Soviet Union must not be allowed to prescribe the agenda of this cosmic meeting of peoples. We must care for Africa enough to desire the best for Africa and to give it the best that we have. And so we are entering the era of the new States. Shall we build the City of God in them, or only a different City of Man?

The building of the City of God in the new African States must be the task of Africans, and particularly of those young Africans who have been introduced to our education and our religion. It is, in colloquial phrase, "over to them." What does this building of the City of God mean? It would be misleading, even heretical, to try to link it up solely with what we sometimes call "spiritual" things. A religion which uses water, bread, and wine for its sacraments cannot divorce itself from material things. Africa lies wide open for development of every kind. Its needs are great and, in the words of Edmund Burke, "all virtue which is impracticable is spurious." An African State which is to take any sort of place in the life of the wider world cannot confine itself to agriculture, but it must inevitably rest to a large extent on agriculture. It is to young Africa that we must look for the development of agriculture, which will not only feed the people but will be of such a nature as to give them something to exchange for the wealth of the outside world, and which will at the same time not destroy those things that are of value in its life.

All life is one. Agricultural man, industrial man, and spiritual man are in essence one man. In planning agriculture, therefore, the African statesman of the future must consider not only the technology of farming but also the whole question of land tenure, and with that the structure of the society which he finds and the best possible structure for the society which he desires to build. These things are intimately connected. There is, therefore, a tremendous responsibility resting on the universities of America and Europe in teaching agriculture to African students. Again and again it must be emphasised that the mere science of agriculture is not enough. It must be linked at all points with social living. Land tenure in particular may prove to be one of the toughest problems which African statesmen of the future have to face. African students cannot, of course, be told what the future structure of African society is to be. That is their work. The days of paternalism are over. They will have to make their own decisions. But they must at least be helped to see on what points decisions have to be made and stimulated to face the questions involved. All education ought to be, and African education must be, education for life as a whole.

No young State will be content to rely on agriculture alone, even on diversified and exchange crops. Rightly or wrongly, every young State wishes to establish industries and will do so, whatever avuncular sermons its leaders may receive from professors or moralists in established industrial States. Here in a sense the West is in a very strong position, for if there is one sphere in which it has been successful, it is that of applied science and technology, and Africans, however suspicious of the West they may be in other respects, come to it with real humility that desires to study the "know-how" of industry. Once again, however, this is not enough. The whole mystery of finance is bound up with industrial undertakings, the principles of taxation, the wage level, and in particular all the problems of urbanisation. The industrial revolution need not create slums, although it usually does. We shall have failed on the one point on which Africa is certain to accept our lead if we divorce industry from spiritual values, just as we shall fail in our missionary endeavour if we drive a cleaving sword between worship and industry. It may be that those universities which are undertaking the training of African students should reconsider, even for men of their own race and colour, the present departmentalisation of thought, even the present secularisation of matters which partly at least belong to the realm of the spirit.

The new rural structure and the new urbanisation must inevitably both impinge on family life. In the highly industrialised area of the Republic of South Africa, family life has been the chief casualty of the African people. There are even areas where illegitimate births are more common than legitimate ones, and though in some cases illegitimacy is more irregular than immoral, family life has been badly split. Above all in this and in many other parts of Africa young men are coming to accept the privileges of sex without its responsibilities, and the man who does not look after his children and the woman who bore them is only half a man, even if he claims to be a great leader. In the Protestant missions the remaining missionary families have an important part to play, for family life is best taught by example. We do not yet know what form of structure African life will ultimately take, but we can safely say that no form will be healthy where the trinity of father, mother, and child is not retained and honoured.

The reference that we have just made to health refers obviously to spiritual and moral health, but there is an enormous work to do to build up physical health in Africa. The toll taken by tropical diseases and by malnutrition is very great. Infantile mortality figures are startling. The trouble, however, is worse than this. Many a man dies in his early thirties because his stamina has been undermined by lack of proper nutrition during his childhood. I think of two cases known to myself in the Republic of South Africa- one of a young man who had just completed his Bachelor of Arts and Bachelor of Laws degree, was qualified to be a lawyer, and was a most promising youth leader; another who had got as far as his doctorate in African Studies and been appointed to a university lectureship. Both of these men died in their thirties. They had not been badly nourished during their years of study, but early malnutrition catches up with one sooner or later. As to tropical diseases, the toll which they take is known to every student of African health. The new States have the right to expect the active assistance of the older countries of the world, even of those who have been forcibly extruded from the new republics. This help can perhaps best be administered through the World Health Organisation. Medical help given through this source can be given without raising issues affecting the old colonial status of these new nations, and it is urgently required.

It would be tempting to spend more time on these and other facets of African life, but having made it clear that the building of the City of God affects physical things, we may perhaps pass on to those more usually classified as intellectual and spiritual.

We have spoken of the universities of America and

Europe which have the immense privilege and responsibility of training African students. We must also think of the building up of university life in Africa itself. There will be a great temptation-indeed it is already only too apparent-to speed up the Africanisation of universities on the continent of Africa to a point where the quality of the staff is sacrificed to national pride. There will also be the temptation to create unnecessary universities in order to minister to the prestige of each new State. It could well be that in ten years time there will be too many universities in Africa chasing too few skilled African university teachers. In building the City of God in Africa we shall need to retain the very best university standards built up through the centuries since universities began. These involve some measure of real independence from the State, so that the university is never a mere adjunct to a political programme, a dispassionate and honest pursuit of knowledge with deep integrity, and the avoidance of gaudy and unreal distinctions as a substitute for true scholarship.

It is not merely practical steps which are needed to avoid the possible dangers of university development in Africa, but also help to African statesmen to understand the theoretical basis of university education. It would be good for them to realise what Jacques Maritain has told us, namely that the State is only one organ of what he calls the body politic, that every other organ has its own autonomy, and that just as Church and family exist independently of the State and not by its permission, so does the university. In this pluralism lies one of the main hopes of truth in the new world.

Even in the older countries, the advance of the welfare state and of socialism and the modification of the tax system with the object of reducing fantastically high incomes has meant that universities must seek their financial support from the government. America is almost the last country in the world where it is still possible for universities to receive huge endowments from private sources. Even in Great Britain, institutions as ancient as Oxford and Cambridge receive a growing measure of support from the State. How much more must this be the case in new African communities where there are few rich men.

British and Continental university leaders are convinced of the need for preserving university independence in the face of these growing subsidies. It can be done, but it requires an effort. African statesmen should somehow be made fully aware of this, not as an African problem, but as a world problem in which Africa shares. Indeed nothing is more important as regards African universities than to help them and those concerned with them to see the university of any nation as part of an international freemasonry of scholarship, with its own independence and its own duties, not a mere important adjunct to the State.

SEVENTY-TWO

From the universities we may look down to the schools and consider the many problems which have to be faced there. We cannot expect that the majority of schools will remain in the hands of churches and missions, even if this were desirable, but it is very important to prevent an unreal secularisation of education. The City of God is after all the City of *God*. Something may perhaps be said for not believing in God, but nothing can be said for accepting God and treating him as unimportant. Faith is an attitude towards all life, and in this formative stage of African education to exclude faith from the schools on the ground of some hazy idea of "tolerance" could be a tragedy. What matters more, however, than formal religious education is the attitude of the teacher. Carlyle once spoke of a stonemason who "broke the Ten Commandments with every stroke of his hammer." We do not want teachers like that, even if they enter their names on the census form as members of a Christian Church.

What is surely called for on the part of those in authority is a certain reverence as well as integrity in dealing with the school system. The State has, of course, the responsibility of running schools and a duty to see that all children attend school, but this does not carry with it the corollary that all schools should be government schools. Here is a point on which the government of the Republic of South Africa made so grave a mistake in the administration of the Bantu Education Act of 1953. Old schools founded by Churches or missionary societies, some of which had been in existence for over a century and had built up great traditions, were ruthlessly taken over and, with an almost complete change of staffing, made to serve the purposes of government educational policy. How much better it would have been if the government of the Republic had built its own schools and created a healthy rivalry between these and the Church schools as to which could provide the best system of education. If ever it had been necessary to close down mission schools, it would have been when all children were at school-a state of affairs not reached in any African nation yet.

The case for the government's taking over all schools can only be supported by the assumption that the duty of the State is to indoctrinate its children. Every conscientious teacher will realise what an intolerable burden it is on the conscience and professional skill of the teacher to be expected to take part in this process of indoctrination. If the new States could avoid the mistakes of the Republic of South Africa, what a good thing it would be.

We come now to government itself, and following on the thoughts to which we have already given expression, we should broaden our conception of freedom and democracy. It is greatly to be desired that every African State should have an utterly independent judiciary, that bench and bar should alike be respected and be worthy of respect. It is desirable too that the civil service in these new States should be professional, independent, and not a place in which to reward inefficient political friends. The City of God is not limited to the Church. It should, so far as human frailty permits, be embodied in the institutions of the State. What we much really desire is true righteousness in government in these new and young and hopeful States.

Here we must come back to the theories of liberalism and democracy in our time. The continent of Europe has produced in recent years two outstanding thinkers on democracy, both of whom were Frenchmen. Bertrand de Jouvenel has taught us that what matters more than the "who" of government is the "what." Not "who" governs, but "what" he does. De Jouvenel claims that as, until recent times, books were written to show Princes how to govern, so now it is necessary to write books to show democracies how to govern. The voice of the people is emphatically not the voice of God. The sanctity of majorities cannot be upheld without reservation by those whose religion is bound up with the tremendous minority of the Cross. Hence de Jouvenel feels that while the process of universal franchise is right and good for its own sake, it is not in itself the end. The question is what the new voters will do and what the statesmen whom they elect will do. The vote, in short, is not a guarantee of infallibility: it is the recognition of the equal moral worth of every man and woman.

Jacques Maritain has told us that it would be a good thing if political scientists could forget the name and even the idea of sovereignty, that the conception of unlimited power is a misleading one. For the greater part of human history men never dreamed of it. No normal mediaeval King had it, nor did any normal African chief. The State, according to Maritain, is only one organ of what he calls the "body politic" but which I prefer to call "society." The trade unions, the university, the Church, the family—all are entitled to their own autonomy, all should have what in British terms we might call their dominion status within the political commonwealth. The combination of Soviet conceptions of the omnipotent State with the British doctrine of the sovereignty of parliament misunderstood and applied in a new context, and the natural lust for power of successful national leaders, could turn Africa into a series of States where all is sacrificed to the political rulers. But this would not be democracy as we have understood and inherited it.

It is probable that de Jouvenel and Maritain have taught the world deeper and more important truths than Marx or Lenin, but their work is hardly known outside a select circle, and I come back at this point to the challenge which

I made earlier in this lecture to American political thinkers. For if America is to exercise the vast influence which she is trying to exercise on the life of Africa, she should know what her faith is–first of all her political faith, and secondly her religious faith.

The political faith is there already, deeply bound up with American institutions and ways of life, but somehow it needs more formulation, more conviction, in order that it may have more influence on emergent Africa. As for our religious faith, the Soviets are not going to be beaten in Africa by people who do not know what they believe or why they believe it. Tepid benevolence is not good enough to meet the Soviet challenge, nor indeed the challenge of Africa even if there were no Soviets. The faith which has to work in Africa today must be utterly dedicated and it must at the same time be selfless. There must be in it both dignity and humility, both patience and trust. Let us make up our minds about it. "If the trumpet give forth an uncertain sound, who will prepare himself for battle?" From us such a faith can be caught by the young leaders of Africa, perhaps more effectively than it can be taught. We must be well equipped for our work, but it is they and not we who will have the real opportunity of building up the City of God in Africa. The truly devoted missionary in the past has realised the truth of John the Baptist's great saying, "Ye must increase and I must decrease," and has applied it to the people among whom he works. Much more so today is it important to realise that they must increase and we must decrease. It does not matter whether we like this or not. Any pride or hurt feelings must be acknowledged, given to God, and left behind us. Whether we like it or not, we can no longer have the primary responsibility for the building up of the spirit of Africa.

In this missionary era, which was also the era of colonisation, we have been able to see that the building of the City of God was accompanied by the building of the City of Man. It has not been easy for Africans to unscramble the mixture. Those who have to work in the new States, the new young African leaders, will be sorely tempted to build their own version of the City of Man along with that City of God which even the worst and weakest in their better moments would desire to erect. There are certain dangers which are bound to beset them, dangers of hatred and suspicion bound up with the past, the dangers of mistaking display for achievement. These are very real dangers. But the worst of all is the danger of self-aggrandisement, the apotheosis of personal ambition, culminating in the leader being worshipped as God. This we know is the heart and origin of sin. It is the worst of human faults. The primal temptation was, "Ye shall be as gods," and the only possible answer to its tragic results was the humiliation of God and His willingness to be a Man. The Messianic tinge which surrounds so much African leadership is a danger which could do immense harm to all the new States of Africa, and it may well ultimately produce under a form of democracy that form of constitution which was once described as "despotism tempered by assassination." With this the Christian Church cannot make terms. It must, if necessary, suffer persecution rather than make terms. This deification of the ruler was the point on which Christianity challenged the mighty Roman Empire. Men went to the fire or to the lions rather than acknowledge the Emperor as God. Let there be no mistake about this. In this the whole genius of Christianity is at stake, and those young African leaders who wish to face the building of the City of God as Christians must face this issue. These words might well be written in blood and blotted with tears as we consider the case of Kikuyu martyrs in East Africa, who died, sometimes under torture, for refusing to take the Mau Mau oath. They were true martyrs and their names should figure in any Christian Calendar of Saints. If many of the successful young men of Africa forget their calling in this respect, there will be those, many of them poor and old, but some of them so young, enthusiastic, and capable that their scruples will mean much, who will have to face persecution if they put Christianity before nationalism. Such is the position of the white man in the Republic of South Africa. If he puts his Christianity before Afrikaner nationalism in that State with its less violent traditions, persecution may merely take the form of exclusion from all important office and possible exile to a distant area or house arrest. In the more tropical and violent parts of Africa death may quite possibly be the portion of such men. The call is a deep and poignant one, and there must be a deep determination in our hearts and a great clarity about the issue. We know that great patience is needed in the young days of a recently liberated State, and perhaps sometimes in the first exuberance of enthusiasm more is said than is deeply meant about the Messianic position of the emergent leader. Nevertheless the issue is plain and clear and not one on which Christians can compromise.

As in the colonisation period there were some white men-alas! too few-who strove to stand for the vision of the City of God which the coming of the white man had brought and to withstand the City of Man which was also brought from Europe to Africa, so now we have the right and duty to ask that some Africans, as they work for the building of the City of God in their new states, will likewise take a stand against the City of Man. To ask for and indeed to expect less from them is to deny them that equality which we truly desire to give them, and to treat them still as children or immature youths.

Having all these things in our hearts we must pray that the new generation of Africa will have the grace and wisdom to discriminate between the City of God and the City of Man, grace and wisdom not to be led astray by the cheap anti-Christian jargon which communism and certain schools of nationalism have introduced into African thought and speech. Communism has not struck deep roots in Africa so far as its positive programme is concerned, but it has had an extraordinary power of destruction and its catch-phrases are widely repeated and half believed.

To us all who have to do with Africa, whether the liberal white man of the Republic of South Africa or the African leader in Nyasaland or Kenya, the call sounds strongly and clearly to make the City of God the supreme loyalty. In the end this appeal transcends race and continents. It is a universal human appeal. With all my heart I make this appeal to myself and to you, and I use this forum to make it to the leaders of the new Africa.

Power has descended on them, as in Augustine's day it descended on Vandal or Frank or Goth. The Roman era of rule ended, as the white man's era of rule has ended. All that the diminishing Romans could do was to pass on to new hands the greatest treasure that they had, and this is the greatest treasure that Europe has. When a father hands on to a grown-up son, he cannot be "paternalistic" if he is to be listened to. But he has the right and duty to tell his son with manliness and humility what has mattered most in life to him. To young Africa, therefore, we hand over this conception of the City of God. We ask young Africa for that utter loyalty which is needed if the City of God is to establish itself.

This is not all. If it were, we should be resting in a higher and less repugnant *apartheid.* In accepting the new States of Africa and Asia we now reach out our hands for help and fellowship. Our world is one world. In it Europe and America have still a very large part to play. The ultimate call is not to establish the City of God in Africa alone, but, as far as may be, in the world of men. This is a reciprocal call. For we can give help to Africa, but we need help from Africa. Our great-grand-fathers often lacked the humility to see this when they went as missionaries to the African continent. They gave much–it would not be an exaggeration to say that in many cases they gave their all. This they did with an ardour and enthusiasm and self-giving which puts us to shame. Never-theless they often failed to see what was good in African life, to reverence it and to learn from it. All was new. They were, as it were, angels from Heaven who had descended into the depths, having nothing to gain, in order to help those who lay in darkness and in the shadow of death. It may have been that in some cases this was the only way in which they could bring their message to Africa: I would not dogmatise about this. Be that as it may, the call to us today is a very clear and simple one, to come with humility and with a real faith that Africa has something to give to the races of the world and to ourselves. We of course always or almost always approach Africans with phrases of courtesy which suggest this. But do we believe it in our hearts? They will soon find us out if we do not. Let us not be unreal about the facts. We do know more in technology and applied science than Africans do. Many fields of learning have been open to us for a long time which are virtually closed to them. But in art in all its forms, including rhythmic art, in worship, in the successful adaptation to life in tropical conditions, and in other fields, we can learn from Africa.

We are called, therefore, to a united effort, with Africa as our equal partner, for the world as a whole. This is a fellowship which cuts across race and transcends continents, which calls together men of diverse religions in the cosmic struggle. We do not know whether we shall succeed as the world reckons success. Indeed no man is armed for life at all unless he is armed to meet the utter ruin of the things he loves most. The issues of Africa are in higher Hands than ours. "This is the victory that overcometh the world, even our own faith."

THREE

THOUGH not formally at war, the Republic of South Africa is in a state of siege. Under heavy, relentless pressure from the outside and threatened with upheaval from within, its citizens, as Dr. Brookes reflects in his next essay, are deeply troubled. Diplomatic and economic pressure is being exerted against their country, and there is the threat from many of the other African states of the resort to military means, if necessary. Indeed, the conference of the heads of African states which met at Addis Ababa in May, 1963, virtually declared war against the country.

EIGHTY-FOUR

South Africa is charged with two offenses which are regarded as very serious by present world opinion, and especially by the newly independent peoples of Africa. Though the whites constitute but a fifth of the total population of the country, only they have political rights. This is colonialism in its worst form, as the Africans see it. The second offense compounds the first. It is the policy of extreme racial discrimination, generally known as *apartheid.*

For an understanding of the peculiar mentality of the whites of South Africa, a brief examination of their history is indispensable. Unlike the Europeans in Kenya and the Rhodesias, the whites in South Africa are not newcomers to the continent. They have lived in South Africa for more than three centuries, and they had settled much of the country before the Bantus pushed down into it from the North. This is an important factor in the situation from the whites' point of view.

There were 3,067,638 white inhabitants in South Africa in 1960, according to the official census of that year. Of this number, roughly 55 percent are Afrikaans-speaking and something less than 45 percent are English-speaking. The former are nearly all descendants of the settlement of about 2,500 persons which the Dutch East India Company established at Cape Town in 1652. Among the early settlers there were a considerable number of French Huguenots and a lesser number of Germans. They became completely absorbed by the Dutch in a very short time. The settlement at Cape Town was not intended to be a colony but a refreshing station for the company's ships on their long voyage to Java, hence there were few accessions from Europe after the early years.

The geographic isolation of Cape Town meant cultural isolation for the European settlers, especially in view of the fact that after the first few decades very few persons came from Europe to join the settlement. This cultural isolation became more pronounced for those large numbers who moved from Cape Town and the surrounding area and pressed farther and farther inland. They acquired the characteristics of the frontiersman, both good and bad. About the only cultural influence in their lives was the church. The Boers, as they came to be called, were a deeply religious people. The Bible and the Reformed Church were not left behind as they trekked far northward and eastward but continued to play a dominant role in their lives. Their interpretation of the Bible, however, became colored by their environment, experiences, and problems. They began to see themselves in a role very similar to that of the children of Israel. They felt themselves called of God to open the northern and eastern regions for civilization and the propagation of the Christian gospel among the inferior heathen.

EIGHTY-SIX

As the Boers trekked eastward and northward they encountered the Bantus, who were moving southward under pressure from tribes farther north. At first an attempt was made to maintain a frontier between the two races, but this proved impossible. In 1779 there broke out the first of the Kaffir or Frontier Wars, a series of hostilities lasting about a century. They were essentially a continuous struggle between two streams of colonists for possession of land. The more highly developed whites won, but the Bantus, unlike the Indians of North America, were too numerous to be exterminated or pushed back. The outnumbered whites became the masters of the blacks. They not only monopolized political power, but also they instituted and maintained a comprehensive and rigid racial segregation.

The Napoleonic Wars brought changes which profoundly influenced the history of South Africa. Britain occupied Cape Colony from 1795 to 1803, reoccupied it in 1806, and acquired sovereignty over it by treaty in 1814. With British rule there came English immigrants, a considerable number of missionaries, and more liberal political and social ideas. The missionaries clashed frequently with the Boer frontiersmen over the treatment of the Bantus by the latter. The trekkers, as they were called, disliked the restraints of any government, as is evident from the difficulty they had in setting up governments in their new settlements, but they especially disliked British rule because it sought to protect the Bantus from the worst practices of the trekkers. They complained that the British government did not give the frontier regions security against Bantu raids, but a more basic reason for their deep dissatisfaction seems to have been the liberal British policy which culminated in the emancipation of the slaves in 1834. This was probably the chief cause of the Great Trek during the years 1836-1854. The Voortrekkers, as these pioneers came to be known, resolved to move beyond the British jurisdiction, establish their own governments, and deal with the Bantus according to their own ideas.

As a result of the Great Trek there finally emerged two Boer states, the Orange Free State and the South African Republic (the Transvaal). Britain annexed the latter in 1877, but restored independence in 1881 after a rebellion which broke out in 1880. The brief war, known among the English as the First Anglo-Boer War but among Afrikaners as the First War for Freedom, fanned the Boer spirit of nationalism which had been slowly developing. With the discovery of diamonds and gold in the territories of the two Boer republics and the influx of large numbers of outsiders, or *uitlanders*, as the Boers called them, conflicts between the British and the Boer governments developed, culminating in the Second Anglo-Boer

War, or simply the Boer War, but which the Afrikaners prefer to call the Second War for Freedom. The War which lasted from 1899 to 1902 ended in the annexation of the two states. The bitter struggle in which two small, farmer republics amazed the world by holding a world empire at bay for a considerable time, intensified Boer nationalism and sharpened the antipathy between Briton and Afrikaner.

At the end of the Boer War it looked as if the cause of the Afrikaner was completely and irretrievably lost. The Boer republics had been wiped out, foreigners, chiefly British, were overrunning the country, and the Afrikaners were broken economically and isolated and stagnant culturally. Yet in less than fifty years the Afrikaners had recovered all they had lost and had achieved a triumph far greater than their defeat. Strangely, at the peak of their achievement and power, they again stand in grave danger of disaster. If the threat is not averted it is likely to engulf not only the Afrikaners but the entire white community in South Africa.

When the early colonists moved away from Cape Town and out of reach of the rigid East India Company control, they began to develop a distinct character. It is in these treks, and especially in the Great Trek, that the genesis of Afrikaner nationalism is to be found. Even in the settled eastern part of Cape Colony a change was taking place. After the first fifty years there were few accessions from the Netherlands, so that the cultural contacts became fewer and less vital. With the transfer of sovereignty to Britain in 1814, practically all ties with the Netherlands were broken. The Boers were now on their own, a distinct people. The shift in the name applied to them is significant. "Boer" is merely the Dutch word for farmer, but "Afrikaner" indicates an inhabitant of Africa. The Afrikaners developed a separate language, Afrikaans. At first it was only a spoken language; in time it became a written language as well. The first book in Afrikaans appeared in 1861. However, Dutch continued as the language of polite society, the church, and the government until some forty years ago. In 1914 Afrikaans was recognized as a medium of instruction in the schools except in Natal. The Reformed Church began to use it in services about 1920, but it was not until 1933 that the first Afrikaans Bible was published. In 1925 Afrikaans replaced Dutch as one of the two official languages of the Union. Since that date it has enjoyed complete equality with English in government and education. There is now a considerable body of Afrikaans literature; its poetry is recognized as having an interesting and distinct quality.

Economically the Afrikaners have been backward. Until

recently they were predominantly farmers. While some were well-off, many were poor. Indeed, South Africa is like the South of the United States; it has a poor-white class, which not so long ago was estimated to constitute about 15 percent of the white population. The Afrikaners were slow to enter the professions or business. Because of their social and economic position, many hold views like those held by the Populists in the United States in the last decades of the nineteenth century. Probably for the same reason many were susceptible to National Socialist propaganda emanating from Germany during the days of Hitler. In recent years, however, the Afrikaners have made great strides forward socially and economically.

It is in politics that the Afrikaners have been most successful. It is one field they have dominated. The two Boer republics were destroyed, but a much larger Afrikaner republic embracing the two early ones and the colonies of the Cape and Natal arose to take their place. How this happened can be briefly told. The story involves three threads: federation, self-government, and native policy.

As early as the middle of the nineteenth century the British saw the desirability of uniting their territories in southern Africa in a federation. Without some kind of overall administration it would be difficult to maintain peace in the region, for a common policy toward the African tribes was an urgent necessity. Later the advantages of a customs union and a common administration of railways became important factors. Alfred, Lord Milner, the British high commissioner, and Cecil Rhodes were ardent federationists. In 1903 a customs union was formed, composed of the four colonies (Cape Colony, Natal, Orange Free State, Transvaal), the three high commission territories (Basutoland, Bechuanaland, and Swaziland), and Southern Rhodesia. The union which came into existence in 1910 went beyond federation. It brought the four colonies under a unitary constitution. Provision was made for the possibility of the admission of the protectorates and Southern Rhodesia to the Union, but because of the union's racial policies the British government was unwilling to transfer these native territories, while Rhodesia in a referendum in 1922 rejected incorporation, probably because the English settlers disliked becoming part of a country in which the Afrikaners were in a majority of the dominant population group, with the possibility that the extreme Nationalist Party might at any time obtain control of the government.

Self-government in South Africa has a strange history. In Cape Colony it enjoyed a slow but steady growth almost from the time it came under British rule until the grant of a responsible ministry in 1872. Natal was made a separate colony in 1856 and was granted a responsible government in 1893. The republics, which had been reduced to colonial status, were accorded the same in 1906. With the formation of the union in 1910 the colonies lost the right of self-government, but the new larger political entity began with a popularly elected parliament and a ministry responsible to it.

The first three prime ministers of the Union were former Boer generals. The first, Louis Botha (1910-1919), was an advocate of conciliation between Afrikaners and English, and his ministry was composed of members of both groups. General J. C. Smuts was closely associated with him. The outbreak of World War I so soon after the Boer War was extremely unfortunate for this policy of seeking to unite Boer and Briton in a South African nation. Botha and Smuts felt that the only decent response to British magnanimity in granting self-government and union so soon after the Boer War was complete loyalty to the empire in the world war in which it had become involved. Though the use of South African troops to wrest South-West Africa from the Germans might be regarded as a thoroughly South African interest, the mere thought of fighting for the empire which had ruthlessly destroyed the Boer republics only twelve years before stirred up diehard Boer animosities. A rebellion broke out, and Botha and Smuts had the painful duty of taking military measures against former war comrades. By these acts Smuts incurred the bitter enmity of many Afrikaners.

When Botha died in 1919, Smuts succeeded him as prime minister. During the war Smuts had become a leading figure in the British Empire and Commonwealth and a world statesman, but this did little to enhance his political strength among Afrikaners at home. General J. B. M. Hertzog, also a former Boer general and a leader of the Nationalist Party, formed a political alliance with the Labor Party, which was composed almost exclusively of English workers. The two parties won a majority of the seats in Parliament in an election in 1924 and formed a coalition government with Hertzog as prime minister. This strange union of Afrikaner nationalists and British labor leaders was brought about, at least in part, by similar attitudes toward the native question. Labor feared the competitive pressure of the nonwhites for jobs and demanded legislation providing for job reservations. However, they were loyal British, and to obtain their cooperation the Nationalists had to promise not to sponsor republican measures so long as the pact, which formed the basis of the coalition, was in effect. Hertzog nevertheless did press for a formal clarification of the status of the dominions. The Statute of Westminster of 1931, which formally recognized the legislative independence of the dominions and gave them undoubted international status, was in no small measure the result of the insistence and leadership of Prime Minister Hertzog at the Imperial Conferences.

The world depression of the nineteen-thirties hit South Africa very hard. To cope with the domestic problems Hertzog and Smuts in 1933 formed a coalition cabinet of six Nationalists and six members of the South African Party, with the former as prime minister and the latter as his deputy. The coalition won an overwhelming majority in the elections held shortly after its formation, and in the next year the two parties fused to become the United Party. A small group of Nationalists under the leadership of Dr. D. F. Malan refused to join in the fusion and continued their identity as the Purified Nationalist Party.

The outbreak of World War II caused a split between Hertzog and Smuts. The former wanted to follow a policy of neutrality in the war, while the latter pleaded for a declaration of war on Germany and cooperation with the Allies. Smuts carried Parliament with him by a narrow majority. He thereupon became prime minister, and Hertzog with most of his followers returned to the ranks of the Nationalist Party. At the end of 1940 Hertzog retired from Parliament and politics. He died in 1942.

After the war the Smuts ministry was beset by numerous

difficulties, domestic and foreign. The refusal of his government to convert the League of Nations mandate over Southwest Africa into a trust territory under the United Nations invoked sharp criticism in the General Assembly of South African racial policies, a criticism which has steadily mounted and has now become a bombardment from nearly every corner of the world. In the election campaign of 1948 the Nationalists made racial policy the chief issue. To the surprise of nearly everybody, including themselves, the Nationalists won 70 of the parliamentary seats to 65 for the United Party of Smuts. The small Afrikaner Party fused with the Nationalists, and Malan became prime minister. For the first time South Africa had a ministry composed exclusively of members of one linguistic group; every member of the cabinet was an Afrikaner.

The Nationalists strengthened their position in Parliament in succeeding elections and moved rapidly to achieve all of the Afrikaner Nationalist goals. More comprehensive and more rigid racial legislation was enacted. In 1950 appeal to the Privy Council in London was abolished; in 1957 the Afrikaans *Stem van Suid-Afrika* was made the sole national anthem; in 1961 South Africa was declared a republic and withdrew from the Commonwealth.

In effect, South Africa has become an Afrikaner republic.

NINETY-SIX

The Afrikaner Nationalists by politics have recovered, and more than recovered, what they had lost by arms sixty years before. Even English-speaking South Africans are now joining the Nationalist Party. In 1961 two of them became members of the Nationalist ministry, which now rules the country with an iron hand.

Thus has been laid to rest one of the two great fears which have haunted the Afrikaner: that the English language and culture would replace his. The other, that the whites might become submerged and disappear "in the black sea of South Africa's non-European population," has become an obsession.

Though the term *apartheid* did not come into general use until the election campaign of 1948, it was nothing new in South African thinking or policy. It may be defined as a development of the traditional policy of white South Africa to save itself and its way of life from being "swamped by the numerically superior, still largely illiterate and relatively primitive Bantu masses." The whites of South Africa have used every means conceivable to maintain their supremacy. Nonwhites are in general denied the right to vote; the Bantus have been deprived of the little representation they once had in the House of Assembly; the Coloureds of Cape Colony may elect four Europeans as their representatives in Parliament. This is the extent of the political participation of the non-Europeans, who constitute four-fifths of the total population. As for the rest, there is the most comprehensive and detailed educational, social, and, as far as the interests of the whites permit, economic segregation. How to take full advantage of the Bantu labor, without which South Africa's large industrial complex could not be operated, and yet protect the white laborer from the competition of the blacks for the better jobs, constitutes a real problem. Job reservation for the whites is a device used, but often it is put to a severe strain.

How difficult it is to maintain this kind of a policy, especially in the face of Bantu educational and economic progress, and what such a policy requires is frankly stated by the son of General Smuts, who, though bitterly hostile to the Nationalists, sees no other alternative. The white man in South Africa is outnumbered four to one and the black man is increasing more rapidly than the whites. Since it is impossible for two peoples to go on indefinitely living side by side in this fashion without a major upheaval, the whites must prepare for a day of reckoning: "We must see that we have in our power all those things which can ensure tactical and military superiority. We must prohibit non-Europeans from possessing firearms, or the training in their use. Manufacturing industry, wealth and education must be kept in white hands. All these add up to military strength. We must frown on trade unionism among the Bantu or upon the formation of political bodies, for that leads to potentially dangerous consolidation."[1]

Logically this policy requires that the natives be prevented from gaining a position from which they can bargain. What the younger Smuts failed to see or to recognize is that this kind of relentless policy requires ever greater suppression which in the end must result in a catastrophic eruption. Moreover, this kind of a policy does grave spiritual injury both to those who impose it and those upon whom it is imposed.[2]

Afrikaner leaders have recognized the difficulty of the native problem. Smuts speaks of it as insoluble, and in this he was probably reflecting his father's views. The elder Smuts rarely addressed himself to the problem directly, and when he did it was invariably in somber tones. In March, 1945, the racial problem came up in Parliament and Smuts discussed it at some length. He frankly stated that he could give no answer to many of the points raised. History would have to give the answer. "It lies in the

[1] J. C. Smuts, *Jan Christian Smuts* (Cape Town, 1952), p. 306.

[2] The dilemma confronting those who impose this policy has been poignantly put by Dr. Edgar H. Brookes: "The longer they wait, the more grudging their concessions, the more terrible their ultimate ruin – an outer ruin – almost complete, if they are beaten; an inner ruin, quite complete, if they win." *The City of God and the Politics of Crisis* (London, 1960), p. 6.

future which is not only dark but endless. . . .We must leave certain replies over to our descendants. We must not take too much on our forks; already we have enough." He then went on to say: "It is a surprisingly difficult task, the most difficult with which we can cope. We have not yet a direction in connection with it on this continent. We are still searching. . . .We have here the boiling pot of racial questions and there is no doubt – I feel it – that this greatest problem of mankind is the problem of race and color, and will remain a question in Africa for many years to come. I do not know whether we will find a solution. It may be that the problem is unsolvable and lies outside the capacity of man. . . .This continent is the continent of racial problems, which is the greatest problem of humanity, and on it depends the whole future of the human race. . . . One cannot solve it but one can approach a solution."[3]

At the conclusion of Smuts' speech the future prime minister, J. G. Strydom, said that as he listened to the prime minister the Bible phrase "almost persuaded to be a Christian" entered his mind. "If the Prime Minister continues in the same vein a little longer he will become a Nationalist." With respect to the racial question, for all practical purposes Smuts' views were not very different

[3]Union of South Africa House of Assembly, *Debates*, vol. 52, col. 3976 (March 22, 1945).

from those of the Nationalists. There seems, however, to
have been at least one difference. Smuts was not sure that
there was a solution to the problem, but the Nationalists
are convinced that there is a solution and that they have it.
But even Dr. Malan, Nationalist prime minister from
1948 to 1954, at times publicly confessed to the extreme
difficulties which beset the problem. In 1926, when he was
minister of the interior, he declared in the course of a de-
bate in Parliament, "South Africa is a land of great, and
we may say, of terrible problems."

By contrast, Dr. H. F. Verwoerd, the prime minister
since 1958, constantly sounds a note of great optimism,
even though to most observers the situation looks increasingly ominous for South Africa. He frequently boasts to
Parliament that there is more law and order in South Africa than in most countries of the world; in his 1963 New
Year message to the country he declared that "a general
spirit of great optimism prevails," but more significantly,
practically every year he asks for more drastic repressive
legislation. In 1963 he asked for and obtained the "no-
trial law," by which police may hold persons without
bringing charges against them for ninety days, and repeat
this indefinitely.

A few figures on the racial composition of South Africa's population will indicate how difficult the problem

of continued white domination is. The country in 1960 had a total population of about 16,000,000, of which about 11,000,000, or over two-thirds, were Bantus; about 1,500,000, or nearly one-tenth, were Coloured, that is of mixed blood; and about 500,000, or about 3 percent, were Asiatics, chiefly Indians. The whites numbered something over 3,000,000, or only about one-fifth of the total population. As the non-Europeans acquire more education, industrial skills, and wealth, it becomes increasingly more difficult to deny them equal political rights with the whites. The principle of "one man, one vote," even if the qualifications for suffrage were set fairly high, would shortly lead to Bantu control of the government. White domination would be replaced by black domination, which is something the vast majority of South African whites, and especially the Afrikaners, refuse to accept, or even to contemplate. As they see it, black domination would mean the destruction of the European civilization which was built up at the foot of the Dark Continent over several centuries at the cost of much toil and sacrifice. It would also mean the absorption of the white race by the black.

The Afrikaner Nationalist has frantically examined every method or device which has offered any hope of strengthening the whites against the blacks. In the past they have been opposed to the encouragement of immigration for the reason that most of the immigrants were either English or, after coming to South Africa, joined the English-speaking section of the population. In desperation the government has turned to an active promotion of immigration. In 1961 an English-speaking senator, A. E. Trollip, was named minister of immigration. He has succeeded in attracting an increased number of immigrants. South Africa received about 20,000 immigrants in 1962, but 9,000 persons left the country. The number of emigrants is high; after an outbreak of racial disturbances and violence the outward stream sharply increases in volume. In three of the years of the 1950-60 decade more persons left the country than entered it. Stimulation of European immigration can do little to increase the relative strength of the whites. The natural increase of the blacks is greater than that of the whites, and black immigration from surrounding countries is normally much greater than white immigration. Indeed, the attraction of South Africa for the foreign Negro is so great that about a million have made their way into the country. This is one of the anomalies of the situation. While the governments of the newly independent states are clamoring to overthrow the white regime in South Africa, many of their citizens are eager to migrate to that country.

Grim logic on the part of the racialists closed the door to a ready means of increasing the relative strength of the whites over against the blacks. By assimilating the million and a half Coloureds and the half million Indians, the whites could nearly double their numbers. But this cannot be done without a breach of the basic logic on which *apartheid* rests, and it was, therefore, rejected even though a very large percentage of the Coloureds are Afrikaans in language and church affiliation. Many Afrikaner Nationalists have agonized over the case of the Coloureds, being torn between conflicting desires and loyalties.

After many years of opposing Nationalist policies without a real alternative, the United Party has come out with a program which it calls "An Ordered Advance to a Race Federation." The United Party now advocates the repeal or amendment of all laws infringing the individual dignity of nonwhites, the assimilation of Coloureds to the whites, and the representation of natives in Parliament with a federation primarily of races but also of territories as the ultimate goal. Each racial group under this federation would have a "defined" share in the central Parliament, the basic rights of individuals, groups, and areas to be protected in a rigid constitution. The reforms would be very gradual. White "leadership" would continue for some time.

The urbanized Africans would first be granted representation in Parliament and, in the beginning, only by whites.

The United Party's moderate, gradualist program holds little attraction for the Bantus, but it undoubtedly frightens the conservative members of the party, many of whom have joined the ranks of the Nationalists. It is difficult to see how this program would work out in practice. If the Bantus were given seats in Parliament in proportion to their share of the population, and they would not be satisfied with much less, they would dominate the central government. There is no way to nullify the political power of two-thirds of the population of the country except by methods that are grossly unfair and undemocratic.

Only two small parties, the Liberal and Progressive, offer a program based on universal suffrage. The program of the former was first based on the principle associated with Cecil Rhodes, that of "equal rights for all civilized men." It would grant the right of suffrage to all persons who had either a common school education or a modest income. These qualifications were dropped in 1960, and for them was substituted the entrenchment in a rigid constitution of a bill of rights enforceable by an independent judiciary. The Progressive Party advocates the right to vote for all who have had a common school education or enjoy a moderate income, own a certain amount of property, or occupy property of a modest value and are literate. Literate adults who cannot meet the other qualifications would be placed on a special role with the right to elect one-tenth of the members of Parliament. To prevent domination of the government by one racial group the Progressive Party proposes the entrenchment in a rigid constitution of a bill of rights, an "antiracial" Senate, and a federal system of government. The Liberals have at present no members of Parliament, and the Progressives only one.

As events in Africa unfolded and one after another of the colonial territories became independent states and the internal and external pressure on the government of South Africa mounted, the Nationalists' leaders came to the conclusion that the line could not be held much longer on *apartheid.* But absolutely unwilling to move the least bit in the direction of a policy which would endanger white supremacy, they shifted to a policy of separate development. In explaining the new policy in Parliament on January 27, 1959, Prime Minister Verwoerd said that South Africa was at the crossroads. It had to decide "whether it would go in the direction of a multi-racial society with a common political life" or whether it would bring about "total separation in the political sphere." His government had chosen the course by which on the one hand "the White man alone retained full rights of government in his area" and on the other the Bantus would be granted "under our care as their guardians, a full opportunity in their own areas to put their feet on the road of development along which they can make progress in accordance with their capabilities." His government desired "to build up a South Africa in which Bantu and Whites can live next to one another like good neighbours and not like people who are continually struggling for domination." These Bantu areas are called Bantustans.

In this speech the prime minister evaded the question as to whether the Bantustans would be granted independence if they desired it. Pressed on this point, he declared on May 20 of the same year: "The standpoint of the National Party is one of striving for a permanently White South Africa, whatever dangers may threaten it, but which is prepared to develop areas in which Bantu control may increase under the guidance of the Whites as guardians, and with the understanding that even though this should lead to Bantu independence we will try by our statesmanship to ensure that this development takes place in such a spirit and in such a way that friendship will remain possible, but without the White man ever finding himself under any form of Bantu control, whether it be in a federation or a union."

This proposal to balkanize the country made a section

of the Nationalist Party unhappy, but Verwoerd argued that white South Africans had to choose between a smaller state "which is White and which controls its own army, its own fleet, its own police and its own defence force, and which will stand as a bulwark for White civilization in the world," or a larger state dominated by the Bantus. There was no other alternative.

In a speech before the House of Assembly on January 25, 1963, the prime minister assured his followers that the process of training the Bantus in self-government would be slow and cautious. "We shall have to guide our Bantu in their self-government of their own areas step by step so that eventually they will be democratic nations and states and not nations or states which, as the result of the over-hastiness we saw in the Congo or in Ghana, will fall into chaos or become dictatorships." This declaration may have allayed somewhat the discontent of many Nationalists at the prospect of the balkanization of the country, but it sharpened the Bantu opposition to it and it caused world opinion to take a more critical attitude toward it. Under the government's program, independence for the Bantustans was only a dim, long-range prospect.

Leaders of the United Party have repeatedly warned the government that its racial policies were dangerously isolating South Africa. Before his death in 1950 General Smuts plaintively issued a melancholic warning: "If there is one country in the world which needs world support it is South Africa.... Here on this black continent we are a small minority always trying to build up a European civilization. We have done so with remarkable success. . . . But we are a small minority on this continent, and one can understand the need for such a minority to have support far beyond its boundaries, world support, the support of reasonable people in other lands too. But by the policy we have now adopted or purported to have adopted as the official policy of this country we make it almost impossible for us to have that sympathy."

These warnings seem to make no impression on the National ministry. When the leader of the opposition, Sir de Villiers Graaf, at the opening of Parliament in January, 1963, pointed to the deepening isolation of South Africa and the rising demand in the United Nations for action against it, Prime Minister Verwoerd replied that of course a small state should seek friends, alliances, even partners, but only if they promoted the national interests and the nation's survival. Friends, alliances, partners were of no use if they did not serve these ends. What was their use "if the price we must pay is the downfall of White government in South Africa, a change-over to a multi-racial state and eventually non-White domination? The downfall of one's nation, the sacrifice of White government in South Africa is a price which cannot be paid for friends and for partners."

The Nationalist leaders must be given credit for sincerity in believing that their policy of separate development offers the white man the certainty of retaining full control over the affairs of his country and the nonwhite national groups the opportunity to develop themselves and control their own destinies without competition. They claim that it is only the National Party "that can justifiably say that it is heading for racial peace"; that it is offering a policy "that will eventually lead to an absence of racial discrimination because it is only when the races are separated and live like neighbors that discrimination will be able to disappear." They are convinced that in time everybody, inside and outside of Africa, will be able to see the justice and the beneficence of this policy.

Even a cursory examination raises difficult questions about the justice and even the possibility of carrying out the program of separate development. Millions of Africans will have to be moved, and in most cases forceably, from the white to the black territories. Urbanized, detribalized Africans will be compelled to move to the Bantu reserves or Bantustans and live under tribal institutions. The great industrial centers will remain in the white areas, but these industries have required millions of Bantu laborers. The government concedes that several million Africans will always be needed to operate the large Western industries, but these Africans will be regarded as "migrant workers." They will have no political rights in the white territories where they work and live. Presumably all of the present rigid and comprehensive social and economic discriminatory laws will continue to be applied to them. They will have political rights in their native Bantustans, in which they have little interest and where they do not live. This would be a strange political anomaly. Whom could this possibly satisfy? Surely neither the "migrant" Bantus nor those living in the Bantustans would find this acceptable.

Furthermore, the present Bantu reserves have been impoverished by overpopulation and overgrazing. In many areas the land is suffering serious erosion. Until the reserves have been industrialized, they can support few if any more people. The government does propose to develop industries on a large scale in the proposed Bantustans. This part of the program calls for such large outlays of money that whites are complaining about it.

The Nationalist program of separate development is extremely vulnerable at another point. It has no plan for

Indianstans or Colouredstans. The Coloured and Indian communities will be socially and to some degree economically segregated. All they can look forward to are advisory councils with probably some power to regulate purely communal matters.

The government is vague about the mutual relations between white South Africa and the Bantustans. Apparently Verwoerd hopes for cooperation in certain spheres such as customs, foreign policy, and defense. He has suggested an arrangement like the Commonwealth. In view of the fact that South Africa withdrew from the Commonwealth because of the hostility of its members to *apartheid*, this is a strange idea.

If all of the other difficulties could be overcome, and they are very formidable, there is still the question whether South Africa will be granted the time required to carry out its program for the creation of the Bantustans. At the rate the pressures against it are developing, this does not seem probable.

It is difficult to ascertain how serious the internal conditions are because of the thoroughness with which the Africans have been sealed off by repressive police measures. The situation must be grave, or the government would not have asked for or have been granted the "no-trial" law which was enacted by Parliament in May, 1963. The thirty-two African states have virtually declared war on South Africa. Not only in the United Nations but in all of the international organizations they are demanding drastic action against the Republic of South Africa. They introduced and succeeded in getting the 1962 General Assembly of the United Nations to adopt by an overwhelming vote a resolution asking its members to break off diplomatic relations, stop all trade, close their harbors and airports to South African ships and aircraft, and prohibit their ships from entering South African ports. Later they petitioned the Security Council to apply sanctions against Portugal and South Africa.

South Africa has been called the Israel of Africa. Just as Israel has been and continues under great hostility from the Arab states, so the Republic of South Africa is subject to great pressure from the African states. There is, however, an important difference. Israel has the sympathy, friendship, and support of many countries, including nearly all of the great powers. South Africa has few if any supporters.

The history of Afrikaners contains strange contradictions and sad changes of fortune. During their desperate struggle for national survival in the war against the British (1899-1902) the Boer republics pleaded for foreign intervention; today the Afrikaner Nationalists bluntly reject all foreign pleas for moderation of their racial policies. Sixty years ago the world applauded their courageous struggle for national survival; today there is almost universal condemnation of their denial of basic human rights to millions of their fellow countrymen. In 1914 the Nationalists opposed the military campaign to free South-West Africa from German rule; today they seem prepared to fight the world to keep it. What they lost by appeal to arms, they have more than recovered by politics; but now at the peak of their triumph they are confronted with the danger of losing all of their marvellous gains. These are the people, his compatriots, whom Dr. Brookes discusses in the next chapter.

FOUR

HAVING previously considered Africa as a whole, we come now to that part of the continent which I know most intimately and most poignantly-the Republic of South Africa. Over it hangs the shadow of impending disaster, yet there are lightning-flashes of hope through the clouds. Few countries are more interesting at the present time in history.

I begin under a serious disadvantage. In my previous chapter I tried to be, within the limits of my power, scholarly and objective. In this, however, the fires burn too close to make impersonality easy, and while I shall try to restrain myself, I must ask your pardon if the first person singular obtrudes itself too much into my handling of the subject, and if deep feelings break through scholarly impassivity.

Have you ever tried to imagine how it must feel to belong to a country which is hated by all the world, attacked regularly in the world's most influential forum, and held up to obloquy on every possible occasion? Can you, in trying thus to stretch your imagination, feel what it must be like to be one of the citizens of such a country who have tried over more than three decades to reform its policies and have been uniformly unsuccessful? Can you further imagine that you are in the position of knowing personally that the citizens of the country attacked have many substantial merits, and that some of its most virulent attackers have themselves records that would not bear scrutiny? This is the position of a liberal-minded citizen of the Republic of South Africa today. If out of this pain I try to tell you of the problems of my country, I hope that I shall have your sympathy and understanding. What I do not want to elicit from you, however, is support of my country's policies, for I do not support them myself, and on the vital issue of the colour-bar South Africa is so clearly wrong and even the worst of her attackers so clearly right that one cannot ask for the attack to be called off. I say this at the outset lest you should think that my love for my fellow-countrymen and my analysis of the historical circumstances which have made them what they are might lead to a dangerous condoning of the Republic's wrong policies. I am in short in the position of a convinced anti-slavery Southern Unionist in 1865, rejoicing at the victory of freedom, but very conscious of the magnificence of Robert E. Lee and those like him, and sorrowing at the destruction of so much that was good in the Old South–a destruction inevitable because of the South's own obstinacy, but sad none the less. *Sunt lacrimae rerum.* Yet man must move on, and time truly "makes ancient good uncouth."

The first settlement of white men in South Africa took place three hundred and eleven years ago–in 1652, before Pennsylvania was established and while New York was still a Dutch colony. The settlers came from a Europe which believed devoutly in the divine right, and indeed the pious duty, of Europeans to colonise heathen lands. They met on their arrival not the relatively advanced Bantu but a much more primitive people whom they nicknamed the "Hottentots." The average Dutch soldier or sailor was not equipped to take a philosophic view of the situation nor to think centuries ahead. To him Hottentots were stinking barbarians and nothing more. The Hottentots on their side were not very receptive to the civilisation of Europe. In 1657 the first slaves were introduced. Thus from the very beginning, colour was equated with ignorance and inferiority. When in the Great Trek at the beginning of Queen Victoria's reign the Afrikaners moved northwards and eastwards, they trespassed on African-held land. The African, retaliating by war and massacre, became "the enemy," the stereotype of a savage and dangerous warrior, much as American frontiersmen once regarded the Red Indian. Even the British occupation, though it led to the abolition of slavery and the reform of legislation affecting men of colour, left the Africans still in many respects an inferior people. Cecil Rhodes in the 1890's did in Mashonaland and Matabeleland, the present Southern Rhodesia, much the same as the Voortrekkers had done in their areas sixty years before. Even in the peace which ended the Boer War on the 31st of May, 1902, the British promised not to introduce a franchise for Africans in the conquered Boer Republics until they had received "self-government," i.e., government by whites alone; and a British Liberal government ratified this in 1906 and 1907. The Union of South Africa, formed on the 31st of May, 1910, began with a colour-bar in the membership of the Union Parliament, and with no non-white voters in the old Republics of the Transvaal and the Orange Free State. Begotten in the era of colonisation, nurtured through racial wars, formed anew by late nineteenth-century imperialism, the Republic of South Africa was exceptionally ill prepared for the liberation movement which followed the Second World War.

The greatest statesman thrown up by the Afrikaner people, Jan Smuts, outstanding personality though he was, did singularly little to prepare his people for the coming storm. General Smuts, whom I had the honour of knowing personally, was undoubtedly a very great man, for whom I still feel deep reverence and admiration. With Louis Botha, he met conquest with magnanimity, learning to work with the British against whom he had fought with tenacious valour. This very unusual Boer general, who went to war with Kant's *Critique of Pure Reason* and the Greek New Testament in his knapsack, was never a mere politician. In his complex personality the tenets of liberal theory had a very high place. He honoured the British Liberals who had restored his country. He, more than any other man, was responsible for the constitution of the Union of South Africa. He was one of the founders of the League of Nations. He played a considerable part in the drafting of the charter of the United Nations. Philosopher, botanist, mountaineer, and humanist, he seems the last man to associate with the present ills of South Africa. His very virtues were against him, for they helped his supporters to feel that any evils which his broad and liberal mind tolerated were really tolerable. Yet all South Africa's present controversies with the United Nations stem from his period of rule. He it was who in the first instance obtained the equivocally worded mandate for South-West Africa and who after 1945 refused to turn it into a trusteeship agreement. He it was who in 1946 imposed new restrictions on Indian land purchase. He it was who, up to the moment of his fall in 1948, failed to face fairly and squarely the issue of the franchise for Africans.

To what are these things to be attributed? How could this great international liberal be in internal matters such a conservative? Note well the answer to this question, for it throws a flood of light on the dilemma of South Africa. The author of the book of Ecclesiastes says: "Two are better than one and a threefold cord is not quickly broken." Most South Africans would accept the first half of the aphorism; few would rise to the second. The three elements of "Bantu, Boer, and Briton"—of African, Afrikaner, and British South African—seem too much for most South Africans to grasp at the same time, to love with the same intensity. What might be a manifestation in human love of the Holy Trinity has become merely an eternal triangle. I have met some South Africans who would stand for Bantu and Briton to the exclusion of the Boer; Smuts was one of those who stood for Briton and Boer at the expense of the Bantu.

Note that this terrible choice is forced on ordinary South Africans like myself all the time. Constantly we have to make heart-breaking choices. For example the Boy Scout and Girl Guide movements have admitted Africans into their organisations; the result is that Afrikaners have hived off and formed a separate organisation, the Voortrekkers. When the National Union of South African University Students admitted students from an African university college, all the Afrikaans-speaking universities seceded to form the *Afrikaner Studentebond*. The liberal attitude of the Christian Council of South Africa on race questions has meant that the Dutch Reformed Churches play no part in it.

In the case of General Smuts there was a special history. After the Boer War he and General Botha threw their whole hearts into the task of conciliation between the Afrikaans-speaking and English-speaking groups. As a result of South Africa's participation in the first World War on the same side as Britain, a strong Afrikaner Nationalist group was formed which seceded from Botha and Smuts and went on growing in strength. When the main English-speaking political party dissolved itself and joined Smuts in 1921, he was placed in the position of representing the British element plus only a minority of the Boer element, and he became almost pathetically anxious to retain the support of his own people, not to become the Boer head of the British. The one point which would have driven most of the rest of his Afrikaner supporters away would have been his espousal of the cause of franchise for Africans. So he temporised, hesitated, and evaded South Africa's greatest issue, in order not to see his life-work of reconciling the two white groups undone.

There are Afrikaner liberals today. There have been in the past. They would have followed a truly liberal Smuts, but they would probably even under his dynamic leadership not have exceeded 5 percent of their group. That the results of Smuts' holding back were evil is not difficult to see; that he, being who and what he was, was wrong in his attitude is not so easy to prove. All the elements of a Greek tragedy begin to gather round this and other aspects of the South African situation.

There were, for example, some elements of real and great value about the white South African people. Let us try to analyse them. It would be well in the beginning to probe the real differences between the Afrikaans-speaking and English-speaking South Africans. There is a widespread view that the Afrikaner is the villain of the piece and that British South Africans are far more liberal in their attitude. This is an over-simplification. Among Afrikaners there are a few outstanding liberals and many men of goodwill. A large proportion of the English-speaking South Africans believe in the colour-bar and would prefer Dr. Hendrik Verwoerd to a liberal prime minister. To realise this, it would be a help to look at Southern Rhodesia. There men of substantially the same stock drove Garfield Todd out of office and, though going further than most English-speaking South Africans have been willing to do, are still far from being liberals.

At the same time there is a difference, for the bulk of the spiritual and intellectual leadership of the British South African is anti-*apartheid*, while that of the Afrikaner is pro-*apartheid*. It would require as much moral courage to support *apartheid* in an Anglican or a Methodist Synod as to oppose it in a Dutch Reformed Synod. The English-speaking universities are in the main against *apartheid*; the Afrikaans-speaking are for it. Did not the Students' Representative Council of the University of Pretoria send fraternal greetings to the white students at Oxford, Mississippi, in their struggle "for the preservation of white civilisation," while the Students Representative Council of the University of Natal cabled its fraternal support to James Meredith? Yet not all the people of Pretoria agreed with their university, nor all the people of Natal with theirs.

With these reservations let us forget about the linguistic and traditional differences within the white South African population and take it as a whole. We shall find in it a handful of courageous men and women willing to go all the way with the non-whites, to agree to universal suffrage and to take the consequences. At the other extreme we shall find many cases of real brutality and injustice, and a vast mass of selfish apathy, of willingness to go on living in extreme comfort on the backs of the toiling Africans. But within these extremes we shall find many men of ability and genuine goodwill. A nation which has produced men like Cecil Rhodes, John X. Merriman, W. P. Schreiner, General Botha, General Smuts, and General James Hertzog is not devoid of political abilities. Its legal record is outstanding. The farms, mines, and industries which have made South Africa a rich country have been the work of white brains and enterprise. To hand all over to a majority of untrained African voters is questionable policy. By many white South Africans it is seen as political death. The Afrikaner in particular, deeply rooted in African soil, having fought the African tribesmen and the British imperialist, having at last "arrived," finds himself (as he sees it) called upon in his hour of victory to yield up at once the harvest of the toiling and suffering centuries to another. He rebels against the thought and has transferred to the United Nations and the outside world generally the persecution complex which he cherished so long against the British Empire. Humanly speaking he will yield only to conquest; conquest will be a long, bitter, and difficult process, and those who survive it will be the survivors of themselves. The chief hope lies in the fact that those little words "humanly speaking" may not be the last words of the discussion, that transcending human institutions the City of God stands in its splendour, and may yet prevail.

Now let us look at the vast majority of South Africans, for these are black and brown, not white, and they are without substantial rights in the land of their birth, condemned to perpetual inferiority by the colour of their skins. The facade of *apartheid* hardly takes in even those who are responsible for it. The proposed new African States like the Transkei will have very limited self-government and will remain in many matters, including foreign relations, war and peace, customs tariffs, currency, and even the preservation of internal order, under the parliament and government of the Republic of South Africa, in which they are totally unrepresented. Apart from that, a large number, probably the majority, of the non-white people of South Africa will remain within the so-called white areas. These comprise the people of mixed races (to whom alone the term "Coloured" is applied in South Africa) who live mostly in the western half of the Cape Province hundreds of miles away from the African reserves, the Indians concentrated largely in the Province of Natal which insistently called in their great-grandfathers to ensure the success of its nascent sugar industry, and finally those hundreds of thousands of Africans by whose labours the great industries of South Africa have been established. To those elements of the population the South African government holds out no hope–only honeyed and unreal words about impossible

Coloured and Indian areas, and a promise to urban Africans of a vote, not where it would be of advantage, in the areas of their employment, but for a small proportion of seats in the distant and limited legislatures of the tribal regions which, at best, are vacation and retirement areas and, at worst, places with which all connection has long been broken off.

There is thus no real constitutional liberty in South Africa for men with dark skins. This fact cannot be explained away. No vote is to be given them except for local governments with limited powers. In the land of their birth they have a permanently inferior status. The amenities offered to them are separate and unequal; even were they separate and equal (which is far from being the case), the very separation would constitute inequality, as the inspired and psychologically sound decisions of the United States Supreme Court have made clear.

Civil liberty they do not enjoy either. Theoretically South Africa is one of those countries where the rule of law prevails, but legislation over a long period of years, the pace of which began to be accelerated as far back as 1927, has reduced this to nothingness in the case of Africans. An African political leader who makes himself a nuisance may be imprisoned for a limited period without trial, may be placed under stringent house arrest for an unlimited period, may, like my friend Chief Albert J. Luthuli, be restricted to one small local area and forbidden to attend public meetings even in that area, may be banished – as over a hundred have been – to some remote rural area of a different tribe and language from his own, compelled to stay there and provided with a pittance insufficient for a healthy life. The courts of the country-which, to do South Africa justice, have in the past and even up to the present day been true defenders of justice in the narrowing sphere left to them-have been closed to such men. They are absolutely at the mercy of a political minister.

If an African wants to seek work, he may not just go out and look for it. He must first get permission to seek work from the registering authority in his tribal area and then from the city in which he wishes to work. Either may be refused. He may not remain for more than seventy-two hours in the city without a work-seeker's permit and is liable to arrest if he does not have it. He may not buy land in his reserves, nor in the city, and only to a very limited degree and under restrictions in a few specially appointed rural areas. His children must go to special Bantu schools controlled directly or indirectly by the government and there study a syllabus of instruction deliberately prepared to fit them for their place in the community. Great Church schools, some with over a hundred years of service behind them, have been arbitrarily closed down. The universities – four in number, including the two largest in the country – which admitted African, Coloured or Indian students, have been forbidden under legal penalties to enroll any more, and this although the university authorities and the white students in these universities protested vigorously against this restriction. In their place the non-whites have been given five university colleges, staffed mainly by supporters of *apartheid*, in which they are separated not only from whites but from other tribal or racial groups; these have been subjected to unheard-of restrictions lest any breath of liberty should get into them.

And if this is the case in the intellectual world, the material world is no better. In a country where agricultural surpluses have become a national problem, where thousands of crates of bananas and rivers of oranges have been destroyed, where dairy products and corn have been persistently exported at a loss, African children are suffering from malnutrition on a vast and terrifying scale; a recent American visitor with expert knowledge found *kwashiorkor* at a Durban hospital worse in its incidence than anything he had seen, even in the East. This is, of course, not planned inhumanity, not part of a plot to kill off the African population: it is simply the lack of sufficient desire and of flowering decision to find some way, against great technical and practical difficulties, especially of transport, to get the food to those who need it.

This is by no means an exhaustive account of the disabilities of men of colour in the Republic of South Africa. Barriers meet them at every turn. Everywhere they find separation and too often contempt. Official propaganda aims at showing that this necessary separation is accompanied by goodwill, but too often the facts are otherwise and form a strange commentary on these claims. For example, a few months ago the minister of justice, visiting Durban and about to be entertained at lunch by the body of advocates of that city, declined to come unless the handful of African and Indian members of the profession were excluded from the meal. At an earlier date the minister in charge of African education publicly instructed his officials not to shake hands with the African headmasters of schools (some of them graduates) with whom they had to work. In a school with a long and liberal missionary background, compulsorily expropriated by the government, serious trouble took place because the teacups used by the African and white teachers in their segregated commonrooms had been washed by an ingenuous African employe in the same sink.

More brutal episodes occur, as where, a few months ago, a prison warder, himself a man of colour, beat a prisoner almost to pulp. The judge in sentencing him expressed the view that an enquiry should be held about the running of the prisons, and expressed wonder that only one man had been put on trial for a crime which must have involved more than one.

A few years back an African climbed through a fence and took a short cut across a railway track. He was accused of trespass. Induced to sign an admission of guilt, he found himself sent off to forced labour on a farm. Clothed in a poncho made of hessian and sleeping on concrete, he finally returned to his home and friends, a few weeks later with impaired health–all for a trivial offence which might well have been overlooked. It is, however, typical of South Africa that, in the same country in which this happened, a newspaper immediately exposed the scandal and the exposure was followed by a public outcry. It is also typical that nothing much seemed to happen as a result of the outcry.

May I cite, before passing to the next point of my argument, an everyday happening which affects myself. I employ a house-servant, a most faithful employe between whom and ourselves exists a deep affection. His wife, who suffers from advanced tuberculosis, is being tended in a hospital built largely by the efforts and financial gifts of the white community. His little son lives twenty miles away with a relative. When his wife has completely recovered, I could house her with her husband by engaging her as a servant at a token wage. (This would otherwise be an offence.) But there is no way whatever in which I could house the little boy without committing an offence at law.

These instances, taken almost at random from a long and sombre record, show what Africans must endure in the Republic of South Africa. The examples are few out of many; they have not been so selected as to display only the worst, and they have (I hope) been given with such moderation as is possible. Is it amazing that, in the face of all this, the political leaders of the Africans and other people of colour should launch schemes for the liberation of their people? They have been met with ruthless, decided, and most efficient repression. The effect of this repression is to silence the more moderate and constructive leaders and leave the field open for wilder spirits to work underground and plan schemes of sabotage. The desire for freedom has been greatly strengthened by events happening to the north, by the realisation that the white man's domination has ceased in northern, western, eastern, and central Africa, that the whole world is condemning it in southern Africa. Hopes such as make the heart sick, patience unrewarded, frustration, and a darkness which shows no way out have settled on many. They feel that only force can give them their heart's desire, and yet the material strength of the government is such as to make the use of force a hopeless proposition; its extremely efficient repression makes a general strike or large-scale passive resistance also impossible.

In the face of all this horror of the City of Man, what is the right way for Christian men, black or white, who wish to establish in my country the City of God? It may be argued that this is a case, if ever there was one, when force is needed and should be used; and this claim must not be denied by me through fear of reprisals by my government on my return, or by anyone else because of their fear of the consequences. What we must rather look at is not the immediate dangers of the use of force to ourselves or to others, but the effect of long continued and bitter force (as it probably would be) on the whole country.

It is not at present possible-it may be one day-that the Afrikaner community will go down without fighting. One of their most moderate political leaders said one day in my hearing when I was still a member of the Senate: "I am prepared to be killed, but I will not commit suicide." If force were used, whether from outside or from inside, it would mean civil war; and even if international forces were landed at strategic points, the nature of South Africa is such as to make a prolonged guerilla warfare possible, as the two Republics of the Transvaal and the Orange Free State showed when they resisted the whole might of the British Empire two years after their capitals and their principal towns had surrendered and most of their railway system had been conquered by the enemy. In such a conflict among the first victims would be, as in the Mau-Mau days in Kenya, the devout African Christians. A very considerable proportion of white Christians would be in immediate danger of internment by their own government. These removed, nationalism, Marxism, tribal ferocity, and the savagery of fear working in white men would indeed enjoy a witches' sabbath. The South Africa that would emerge would be a country impoverished and materially weakened to the point almost of ruin, much like the South in 1865. What matters more, it would be set back culturally and intellectually, and its moral and spiritual life would be grievously harmed. In almost every way, except indeed (a notable exception) in the opportunity of ruling themselves, the Africans would be worse off than they are today. They might well feel that no price was too high to pay for freedom, but it would be an immense price. The long saga of the Afrikaner would have ended in total and irremediable failure. His sun would have set. If indeed he could be persuaded to find his inspiration in self-sacrifice rather than self-preservation, if he could voluntarily share with the African, this loss of domination could be the most glorious thing in his tumultuous history. But if it is all forced upon him, there would be nothing to lighten the darkness.

Yet if it happened, we might yet in time rebuild like Ezra the house of the Lord in our country, we might learn from our misfortunes, and though as then the old men might weep as they saw the second temple and remembered the first, the young men might now as in those days rejoice and all might hear some prophetic voice saying: "The glory of this latter house shall be greater than the former, saith the Lord of hosts, and in this place will I give peace, saith the Lord of hosts."

So as always in Christian thought hope flourishes out of despair, for Christ can never be conquered. But should we not try, if we can, to save our land and country from this fiery trial? As Christians we should do so if we can, not because all force is wrong, but because the kind of force which would be needed in South Africa can most easily be roused by preaching hatred, and it is much easier to arouse hatred than to extinguish it.

But if it is dangerous to appeal to force, it is also dangerous to delay. The situation worsens every year, one could almost say every month. Have we any reason to think that, if patience could be maintained for a few more years, things would improve?

One of the sources of hope is the growth of an insurgent minority in the Dutch Reformed Church. As the Church of the majority of voters in the Republic, this hitherto conservative religious body has a strategic position of obvious importance. For a long time now there have been signs that many of its ministers, especially its younger ministers, are searching their consciences and asking themselves how far the present race policies of South Africa are reconcilable with the Gospel. Some two years ago a number of them published a book, *Vertraaide Aksie* (Delayed Action), highly critical of the colour-bar. More recently a periodical on similar lines, *Pro Veritate*, has been brought into being. Of the reality and sincerity of this movement there can be no doubt. Whether it is numerous enough or dynamic enough to bring about changes before they are forced on South Africa is more open to doubt.

Another favourable factor is the length of time during which black and white have been working together. This is greater in the Republic than in any other African territory. Friendships have been formed, and even at this eleventh hour there is a very considerable fund of goodwill and common sense on both sides of the colour line.

Of this there is no doubt, but perhaps it is not as good as it looks. For the experience of Africa generally is that public political demands are often more extreme than personal attitudes. While "A" and "B" can get along together very well and arrive at considerable agreement in private, "A" will almost invariably in public make demands with which "B" finds it difficult or impossible to agree, and one of the most disquieting things to anyone who lives in South Africa is the widening gap between the least which an influential African leader can accept and the most which an influential white leader can concede.

I have used the verb "can" rather than "will" because of the extent of intimidation which often prevents political leaders of conciliatory temper from coming to agreement. Intimidation is rife on both sides. A Dutch Reformed minister, for example, coming out boldly against *apartheid* is bound to have the most serious opposition from his *kerkraad* (church council) and may be forced to resign his pastorate. A recent persecution of a theological professor for heresy was thought to have been really motivated by political dislike of his liberal views. When a group of less conservative members of the United Party (the official Opposition) seceded because they wished to fight for some form of non-white franchise, they were persecuted by the Party with vindictive ruthlessness and all but one lost their seats in Parliament. On the other side an African leader is doomed politically among his people if he expresses willingness to accept, even as a temporary measure, anything less than universal suffrage. So the protagonists are prevented from finding a common meeting ground, and the situation becomes really impossible.

To an impossible situation there is no answer, except an appeal to God with Whom all things are possible. To this Higher Court we must turn for help. And surely as we bring our dying hopes and our very living fears before it, there is one clear answer. Judgement may be given unexpectedly, help may come in unforeseen ways, but in the meantime there is the call to do our daily duty. Prosaic though this may seem, duty carried to the nth degree has all the glory of poetry.

> He that walks it, only thirsting
> For the right, and learns to deaden
> Love of self, before his journey closes,
> He shall find the stubborn thistle bursting
> Into glossy purples, which outredden
> All voluptuous garden roses.

What that duty means in a country like South Africa is to know and to feel the facts, to think with integrity, and to speak with courage. These are not such common virtues as might be imagined. Facts are not always readily available. We may remember that there were Germans who claimed to know nothing of Hitler's concentration camps. Moreover, to know the facts is not enough if they are merely impersonal or statistical; they must be felt with the heart. To think with integrity is not always easy in a country which has, as one writer has put it, cherished the "lie in the soul." From the inescapable conclusions of thought many white South Africans turn in panic. The facts cannot be faced; they are just too terrible to be faced. So a mental picture is painted which is not true, but so much more comforting than the truth. Much of the propaganda for *apartheid* is of this type. Areas are demarcated which are inadequate for the population which they are to hold. Their economic potentialities are exaggerated. The readiness of the people remaining in the "white areas" to accept permanent defranchisement is not questioned. This is not truth; it is in effect one vast lie. The whole picture is a grim *Alice in Wonderland.*

When the devastating truth is seen, the good citizen must speak out. Since this may involve him in imprisonment or in house arrest accompanied by a complete bond of silence, this is not easily done. Yet it must be done, and the risk taken, since otherwise intimidation will have won the day against truth.

There are other forces which operate against the truth. We who are in the struggle are often tempted to assent to what we feel is wrong because we cannot see any alternative answer that is right. But we must never agree to what we feel is wrong. We must have courage enough to say all that we are convinced is right, and integrity enough to say no more than what we are convinced is right.

Daily duty, finally, means that in our profession or vocation we must work creatively, never at any time forgetting that South Africa is a country of 15,000,000 people, not of 3,000,000 whites, using every opportunity in our work for true friendship with men of other races and colours, building love in a world of fear and resentment, hoping for better days.

When all this is done we may, and very likely shall, fail. South Africa as we have known it may disappear from the face of the earth, or be terribly changed for the worse. Success is not entailed to us.

But what is this talk of failure? Our loyalty is not to South Africa. Here we have no abiding City. Our only ultimate loyalty, demanding a self-giving without limits and without reserves, is loyalty to the City of God.

That is a loyalty to things which cannot die, which no revolution can overturn and no sorrow can erode. It is a loyalty to beauty and goodness, to integrity of spirit, to courage and to life. In the last resort it is loyalty to love, unconquerable, self-giving, and redemptive. This is our country, and allegiance to it is our patriotism. Perish South Africa if but the Cross stands and is made glorious in our hearts. This is the consolation which St. Augustine found as the Roman Empire crumbled about him. This he made the inspiration of faithful men for sixteen centuries, and it is alive today. Here at least we cannot go wrong. Here is sureness in the mists of uncertainty. Whoever is loyal to this can never fail.

I have bared my heart to you, not hiding my weaknesses, doubts, and fears, but I end with this affirmation of triumphant faith. If it may one day be made to live in my country, how wonderful that will be! If not, it is still life's ultimate truth and final loyalty.